N/K/K
2005

## ⇜ *Presented to* ⇝

_____

_____

*by*

_____

_____

*on*

_____

_____

*Make your ways known to me, O LORD,
and teach me your paths.*
PSALM 25:4

# Words of Praise

WORLD PUBLISHING

Grand Rapids, Michigan 49418 U.S.A.

Library of Congress Catalog Card Number 95-61695

Published by:   World Publishing, Inc.
                Grand Rapids, Michigan 49418 U.S.A.
                All rights reserved.

Developed and produced by The Livingstone Corporation. Project staff
include: James C. Galvin, Christopher D. Hudson, Michael Kendrick,
Daryl J. Lucas, Kathleen Ristow, and Thomas Ristow. Cover design by
JMK Associates.

ISBN 0-529-10467-9

1 2 3 4 5 6 7 8 9 99 98 97 96 95

# Preface

The goal of this special edition of *Psalms* and *Proverbs* is to communicate the beauty, praise and wisdom of the poetry within the Bible and its relevance to your life today. To accomplish this goal, the translation team of God's Word to the Nations Bible Society used natural, contemporary English. This translation, called GOD'S WORD, will speak to you whether you are well-versed in Scripture or a first-time Bible reader. GOD'S WORD will speak to you whether you are an adult or a child.

Full-time Bible scholars and English reviewers worked together on this translation. Because of the involvement of Bible scholars, this collection of *Psalms* and *Proverbs* is an accurate, trustworthy translation of the Hebrew Masoretic text. Because of the involvement of full-time English reviewers, this collection looks and reads like contemporary poetry.

The poetry in GOD'S WORD is presented in a single-column format to show the parallel thoughts in parallel lines of poetry. The various indentations of the poetry lines indicate the relationship of one line to the others in the same context. These features will help you appreciate the Bible's poetry in English in much the same way as a person reading it in the original languages would have appreciated it.

Since many Bible passages apply to all people, GOD'S WORD uses gender-neutral language so that all readers may apply these passages to themselves.

This translation of *Psalms* and *Proverbs* is uniquely readable and understandable because of careful word choice, single-column format, and an inviting poetic format.

The translation team and support staff of the Bible Society pray that your reading of these poems makes them come to life for you.

For more details on the translation process of GOD'S WORD contact

> God's Word to the Nations Bible Society
> 22050 Mastick Road
> Cleveland, Ohio 44126

# How to Use
# *Words of Praise*

Welcome to *Words of Praise: Daily Inspirations from Psalms and Proverbs*. This special edition of GOD'S WORD has been carefully prepared to help bring you closer to God.

*Words of Praise* is arranged into 90 daily Bible readings. This arrangement enables you to complete the readings at a comfortable, unhurried pace of about three months.

The readings are organized to be convenient and easy to follow. For example, at the beginning of each reading you will find the title Day 1, Day 2, and so on, rather than a date. This way you can begin reading on any day of the year, whenever you're ready.

Each day's reading contains a portion from *Psalms* and a portion from *Proverbs*. The *Psalms* are a collection of song lyrics that give praise and worship to God. The *Proverbs* are a collection of wise sayings.

Here are some tips for getting the most out of God's *Words of Praise*:

1. Before you begin, find a quiet place and time.
2. Begin with a short time of prayer, asking God to speak to you through his Word.

3. Read at your own pace, slowly enough to take in what you're reading.
4. End with a time of prayer, asking God to keep his words with you throughout that day.

Down through the centuries, the books of Psalms and Proverbs have introduced countless people to the love and majesty of God. May this edition of GOD'S WORD, Words of Praise, help bring you closer to him as well.

# Day 1

## PSALM 1

1. Blessed is the person who does not
       follow the advice of wicked people,
           take the path of sinners,
               or join the company of mockers.
2. Rather, he delights in the teachings of the LORD
       and reflects on his teachings day and night.
3. He is like a tree planted beside streams—
       a tree that produces fruit in season
           and whose leaves do not wither.
   He succeeds in everything he does.[a]

4. Wicked people are not like that.
   Instead, they are like husks
       that the wind blows away.
5.     That is why wicked people will not be able
           to stand in the judgment
       and sinners will not be able to stand
           where righteous people gather.

6. The LORD knows the way of righteous people,
       but the way of wicked people will end.

## PSALM 2

1. Why do the nations gather together?
   Why do their people devise useless plots?
2.     Kings take their stands.

---

[a] 1:3 Or "and its leaves do not wither, and whatever it produces thrives."

Rulers make plans together
    against the LORD and against his Messiah[a]
        by saying,

3         "Let's break apart their chains
        and shake off their ropes."

4  The one enthroned in heaven laughs.
The Lord makes fun of them.

5     Then he speaks to them in his anger.
    In his burning anger he terrifies them by saying,

6         "I have installed my own king on Zion,
        my holy mountain."

7  I will announce the LORD's decree.
He said to me:
    "You are my Son.
        Today I have become your Father.

8         Ask me, and I will give you the nations
        as your inheritance
        and the ends of the earth
        as your own possession.

9         You will break them with an iron scepter.
        You will smash them to pieces
        like pottery."

10  Now, you kings, act wisely.
Be warned, you rulers of the earth!

11     Serve the LORD with fear, and rejoice
    with trembling.

12     Kiss the Son, or he will become angry
        and you will die on your way
        because his anger will burst into flames.
Blessed is everyone who takes refuge in him.

---

[a] 2:2 Or "anointed one."

## PSALM 3

A psalm by David when he fled from his son Absalom.

¹ O LORD, look how my enemies have increased!
    Many are attacking me.
² Many are saying about me,
        "Even with God ˌon his sideˌ,
            he won't be victorious."              *Selah*

³ But you, O LORD, are a shield that surrounds me.
    You are my glory.
    You hold my head high.

⁴ I call aloud to the LORD,
    and he answers me from his holy mountain. *Selah*
⁵ I lie down and sleep.
    I wake up again because the LORD continues
        to support me.
⁶ I am not afraid of the tens of thousands
    who have taken positions against me on all sides.

⁷ Arise, O LORD!
    Save me, O my God!
        You have slapped all my enemies in the face.
        You have smashed the teeth of wicked people.
⁸ Victory belongs to the LORD!
    May your blessing rest on your people.      *Selah*

## PROVERBS 1:1-7

### The Reasons for Proverbs

¹ The proverbs of Solomon, David's son who was king
        of Israel, ˌgivenˌ
² to grasp wisdom and discipline,

> to understand deep thoughts,
> 3   to acquire the discipline of wise behavior—
>     righteousness and justice and fairness—
> 4   to give insight to gullible people,
>     to give knowledge and foresight to the young—
> 5    a wise person will listen and continue to learn,
>      and an understanding person
>       will gain direction—
> 6   to understand a proverb and a clever saying,
>     the words of wise people and their riddles.

> 7   The fear of the LORD is the beginning of knowledge.
>    Stubborn fools despise wisdom and discipline.

# *Day 2* ≈

## PSALM 4

For the choir director; with stringed instruments;
a psalm by David.

> 1   Answer me when I call, O God of my righteousness.
>     You have freed me from my troubles.
>    Have pity on me, and hear my prayer!

> 2   You important people,
>     how long are you going to insult my honor?
>     How long are you going to love what is empty
>      and seek what is a lie?      *Selah*
> 3   Know that the LORD singles out godly people
>     for himself.
>     The LORD hears me when I call to him.

4    Tremble and do not sin.
     Think about this on your bed
          and remain quiet.                    *Selah*
5    Offer the sacrifices of righteousness
          by trusting the LORD.

6  Many are saying, "Who can show us anything good?"
          Let the light of your presence shine on us, O LORD.
7       You put more joy in my heart
               than when their grain and new wine increase.
8  I fall asleep in peace the moment I lie down
          because you alone, O LORD, enable me
               to live securely.


## PSALM 5

For the choir director; for flutes; a psalm by David.

1  Open your ears to my words, O LORD.
     Consider my innermost thoughts.
2  Pay attention to my cry for help, my king
          and my God,
          because I pray only to you.
3       In the morning, O LORD, hear my voice.
          In the morning I lay my needs in front of you,
               and I wait.

4  You are not a God who takes pleasure in wickedness.
     Evil will never be your guest.
5       Those who brag cannot stand in your sight.
   You hate all troublemakers.
6  You destroy those who tell lies.
     The LORD is disgusted with bloodthirsty
          and deceitful people.

7    But I will enter your house
          because of your great mercy.
     Out of reverence for you, I will bow
          toward your holy temple.
8    O LORD, lead me in your righteousness
          because of those who spy on me.
     Make your way in front of me smooth.

9    Nothing in their mouths is truthful.
          Destruction comes from their hearts.
              Their throats are open graves.
                  They flatter with their tongues.

10   Condemn them, O God.
          Let their own schemes be their downfall.
          Throw them out for their many crimes
              because they have rebelled against you.
11   But let all who take refuge in you rejoice.
          Let them sing with joy forever.
          Protect them, and let those who love your name
              triumph in you.
12            You bless righteous people, O LORD.
              Like a large shield, you surround them
                  with your favor.

## PSALM 6

For the choir director; with stringed instruments, on the
*sheminith;*[a] a psalm by David.

1    O LORD, do not punish me in your anger
          or discipline me in your rage.
2    Have pity on me, O LORD, because I am weak.

---

[a] 6:1 Unknown musical term.

Heal me, O Lord, because my bones shake
        with terror.
3    My soul has been deeply shaken with terror.
But you, O Lord, how long. . .?

4   Come back, O Lord.
Rescue me.
Save me because of your mercy!
5       In death, no one remembers you.
        In the grave, who praises you?

6   I am worn out from my groaning.
My eyes flood my bed every night.
I soak my couch with tears.
7   My eyes blur from grief.
        They fail because of my enemies.

8   Get away from me, all you troublemakers,
        because the Lord has heard the sound
                of my crying.
9           The Lord has heard my plea for mercy.
            The Lord accepts my prayer.
10  All my enemies will be put to shame
        and deeply shaken with terror.
        In a moment they will retreat
            and be put to shame.

## PROVERBS 1:8-19

### Listen to Wisdom

8    My son,
        listen to your father's discipline,
            and do not neglect your mother's teachings,

9         because discipline and teachings
           are a graceful garland on your head
             and a ⌐golden⌐ chain around your neck.

10 My son,
      if sinners lure you, do not go along.
11     If they say,
        "Come with us.
           Let's set an ambush to kill someone.
           Let's hide to ambush innocent people
             for fun.
12          We'll swallow them alive like the grave,
            like those in good health who go
               into the pit.
13          We'll find all kinds of valuable possessions.
         We'll fill our homes with stolen goods.
14        Join us.
         We'll split the loot equally."

15 My son,
      do not follow them in their way.
      Do not even set foot on their path,
16         because they rush to do evil
          and hurry to shed blood.
17            It does no good to spread a net
             within the sight of any bird.
18 But these people set an ambush
      for their own murder.
      They go into hiding only to lose their lives.
19 This is what happens to everyone
      who is greedy for unjust gain.
        Greed takes away his life.

# *Day 3* ≈

## PSALM 7

A *shiggaion*[a] by David; he sang it to the LORD about the ⸢slanderous⸣ words of Cush, a descendant of Benjamin.

1   O LORD my God, I have taken refuge in you.
    Save me, and rescue me from all
        who are pursuing me.
2       Like a lion they will tear me to pieces
        and drag me off with no one to rescue me.

3   O LORD my God,
        if I have done this—
            if my hands are stained with injustice,
4           if I have paid back my friend with evil
                or rescued someone who has no reason
                    to attack me—[b]
5   then let the enemy chase me and catch me.
    Let him trample my life into the ground.
    Let him lay my honor in the dust.                    *Selah*

6   Arise in anger, O LORD.
    Stand up against the fury of my attackers.
    Wake up, my God.[c]
        You have already pronounced judgment.
7           Let an assembly of people gather around you.
            Take your seat high above them.

---

[a] 7:1 Unknown musical term.   [b] 7:4 Hebrew meaning of this line uncertain.   [c] 7:6 Greek; Masoretic Text "Wake up to me."

8 The LORD judges the people of the world.
   Judge me, O LORD,
      according to my righteousness,
      according to my integrity.

9 Let the evil within wicked people come to an end,
      but make the righteous person secure,
         O righteous God who examines thoughts
            and emotions.
10 My shield is God above,
      who saves those whose motives are decent.

11 God is a fair judge,
      a God who is angered by injustice every day.
12         If a person does not change,
               God sharpens his sword.
            By bending his bow, he makes it ready
               to shoot.
13             He prepares his deadly weapons
                  and turns them into flaming arrows.
14 See how that person conceives evil,
      is pregnant with harm,
         and gives birth to lies.
15 He digs a pit and shovels it out.
      Then he falls into the hole
         that he made for others.
16 His mischief lands back on his own head.
   His violence comes down on top of him.

17 I will give thanks to the LORD for his righteousness.
   I will make music to praise the name
      of the LORD Most High.

## PSALM 8

For the choir director; on the *gittith*;[a] a psalm by David.

1   O LORD, our Lord, how majestic is your name
       throughout the earth!

    Your glory is sung above the heavens.[b]
2   From the mouths of little children and infants,
       you have built a fortress against your opponents
         to silence the enemy and the avenger.

3   When I look at your heavens,
       the creation of your fingers,
       the moon and the stars
         that you have set in place—
4       what is a mortal that you remember him
         or the Son of Man that you take care of him?
5       You have made him a little lower than yourself.
       You have crowned him with glory and honor.
6       You have made him rule
         what your hands created.
       You have put everything under his control:
7         all the sheep and cattle, the wild animals,
8         the birds, the fish,
         whatever swims in the currents of the seas.

9   O LORD, our Lord, how majestic is your name
       throughout the earth!

## PROVERBS 1:20-33

20   Wisdom sings her song in the streets.
       In the public squares she raises her voice.

---

[a] 8:1 Unknown musical term.    [b] 8:1 Hebrew meaning of this line uncertain.

21     At the corners of noisy streets she calls out.
        At the entrances to the city she speaks her words,
22        "How long will you gullible people
           love being so gullible?
       How long will you mockers find joy
           in your mocking?
       How long will you fools hate knowledge?

23        "Turn to me when I warn you.
           I will generously pour out my spirit for you.
           I will make my words known to you.

24        "I called, and you refused to listen.
       I stretched out my hands to you,
           and no one paid attention.
25           You ignored all my advice.
          You did not want me to warn you.
26        I will laugh at your calamity.
       I will make fun of you
          when panic strikes you,
27           when panic strikes you like a violent storm,
          when calamity strikes you like a wind storm,
          when trouble and anguish come to you.

28        "They will call to me at that time,
           but I will not answer.
       They will look for me, but they will not find me,
29            because they hated knowledge
           and did not choose the fear of the LORD.
30        They refused my advice.
       They despised my every warning.
31        They will eat the fruit of their lifestyle.
       They will be stuffed with their own schemes.

| 32 | "Gullible people kill themselves |
|    |     because of their turning away. |

"Gullible people kill themselves
        because of their turning away.
Fools destroy themselves
        because of their indifference.
<sup>33</sup> But whoever listens to me will live
        without worry
        and will be free from the dread of disaster."

# *Day 4* ≈

## PSALM 9

For the choir director; according to *muth labben;*[a]
a psalm by David.[b]

<sup>1</sup> I will give ⌊you⌋ thanks, O LORD, with all my heart.
   I will tell about all the miracles you have done.
<sup>2</sup> I will find joy and be glad about you.
   I will make music to praise your name, O Most High.

<sup>3</sup> When my enemies retreat, they will stumble
        and die in your presence.
<sup>4</sup>   You have defended my just cause:
        You sat down on your throne as a fair judge.
<sup>5</sup>   You condemned nations.
        You destroyed wicked people.
        You wiped out their names forever and ever.
<sup>6</sup> The enemy is finished—in ruins forever.
        You have uprooted their cities.
        Even the memory of them has faded.

---

[a] 9:1 Or *"almuth labben"*; unknown musical term.   [b] 9:1 Some Hebrew manuscripts, Greek, and Latin treat Psalms 9 and 10 as one psalm.

7 Yet, the LORD is enthroned forever.
He has set up his throne for judgment.
8 He alone judges the world with righteousness.
He judges ⸤its⸥ people fairly.
9 The LORD is a stronghold for the oppressed,
a stronghold in times of trouble.
10 Those who know your name trust you, O LORD,
because you have never deserted
those who seek your help.

11 Make music to praise the LORD,
who is enthroned in Zion.
Announce to the nations what he has done.
12 The one who avenges murder
has remembered oppressed people.
He has never forgotten their cries.
13 Have pity on me, O LORD.
Look at what I suffer because of those who hate me.
You take me away from the gates of death
14 so that I may recite your praises one by one
in the gates of Zion
and find joy in your salvation.

15 The nations have sunk into the pit they have made.
Their feet are caught in the net
they have hidden ⸤to trap others⸥.
16 The LORD is known by the judgment
he has carried out.
The wicked person is trapped
by the work of his own hands.          *Higgaion Selah*
17 Wicked people, all the nations who forget God,
will return to the grave.
18 Needy people will not always be forgotten.

Nor will the hope of oppressed people
    be lost forever.
19 Arise, O LORD.
    Do not let mortals gain any power.
    Let the nations be judged in your presence.
20     Strike them with terror, O LORD.
    Let the nations know that they are ˌonlyˌ mortal.
                                  *Selah*

## PROVERBS 2:1-11

### The Benefit of Wisdom

1 My son,
    if you take my words ˌto heartˌ
      and treasure my commands within you,
2     if you pay close attention to wisdom,
      and let your mind reach for understanding,
3     if indeed you call out for insight,
    if you ask aloud for understanding,
4     if you search for wisdom as if it were money
      and hunt for it as if it were hidden treasure,
5     then you will understand the fear of the LORD
      and you will find the knowledge of God.
6     The LORD gives wisdom.
      From his mouth come knowledge
        and understanding.
7       He has reserved priceless wisdom
        for decent people.
He is a shield for those who walk in integrity
8       in order to guard those on paths of justice
        and to watch over the way of his godly ones.

<sup>9</sup>    Then you will understand what is right
and just and fair—
every good course ˌin lifeˌ.

<sup>10</sup>    Wisdom will come into your heart.
Knowledge will be pleasant to your soul.

<sup>11</sup>    Foresight will protect you.
Understanding will guard you.

# Day 5 &#x2766;

## PSALM 10

<sup>1</sup>  Why are you so distant, LORD?
Why do you hide yourself in times of trouble?

<sup>2</sup>  The wicked person arrogantly
pursues oppressed people.
He will be caught in the schemes that he planned.

<sup>3</sup>  The wicked person boasts about his selfish desires.
He blesses robbers, but he curses the LORD.

<sup>4</sup>  He turns up his nose ˌand saysˌ, "God doesn't care."
His every thought ˌconcludesˌ, "There is no God."

<sup>5</sup>  He always seems to succeed.
Your judgments are beyond his understanding.
He spits at all his opponents.

<sup>6</sup>  He says to himself, "Nothing can shake me.
I'll never face any trouble."

<sup>7</sup>  His mouth is full of cursing, deception,
and oppression.
Trouble and wrongdoing are on the tip
of his tongue.

8      He waits in ambush in the villages.
           From his hiding places he kills innocent people.
       His eyes are on the lookout for victims.
9      He lies in his hiding place like a lion in his den.
       He hides there to catch oppressed people.
       He catches oppressed people
           when he draws them into his net.
10     ‚His‚ victims are crushed.
           They collapse,
               and they fall under ‚the weight of‚ his power.
11     He says to himself,
           "God has forgotten.
               He has hidden his face.
               He will never see it!"

12  Arise, O LORD!
        Lift your hand, O God.
        Do not forget oppressed people!
13          Why does the wicked person despise God?
            Why does he say to himself,
                "God doesn't care"?
14  You have seen ‚it‚; yes, you have taken note
            of trouble and grief
        and placed them under your control.
            The victim entrusts himself to you.
    You alone have been the helper of orphans.
15          Break the arm of the wicked and evil person.
            Punish his wickedness until you find no more.

16  The LORD is king forever and ever.
        The nations have vanished from his land.
17  You have heard the desire of oppressed people,
            O LORD.
    You encourage them.

You pay close attention to them
<sup>18</sup>    in order to provide justice for orphans
and oppressed people
so that no mere mortal will terrify them again.


## PSALM 11

For the choir director; by David.

<sup>1</sup>  I have taken refuge in the LORD.
How can you say to me:
"Flee to your mountain like a bird?
<sup>2</sup>      Wicked people bend their bows.
They set their arrows against the strings
to shoot in the dark at people
whose motives are decent.
<sup>3</sup>      When the foundations ˌof lifeˌ are undermined,
what can a righteous person do?"

<sup>4</sup>  The LORD is in his holy temple.
The LORD's throne is in heaven.
His eyes see.
They examine Adam's descendants.
<sup>5</sup>  The LORD tests righteous people,
but he hates wicked people and the ones
who love violence.
<sup>6</sup>      He rains down fire and burning sulfur
upon wicked people.
He makes them drink from a cup filled
with scorching wind.
<sup>7</sup>  The LORD is righteous.
He loves a righteous way of life.
Decent people will see his face.

## PROVERBS 2:12-22

12 Wisdom will save you
    from the way of evil,
    from the person who speaks devious things,
13     from those who abandon the paths
        of righteousness
      to walk the ways of darkness,
14     from those who enjoy doing evil,
    from those who find joy in the deviousness of evil.
15       Their paths are crooked.
      Their ways are devious.

16 Wisdom will also save you
    from an adulterous woman,
    from a loose woman with her smooth talk,
17     who leaves her husband,
        the closest friend of her youth,
      and forgets her marriage vows to her God.
18       Her house sinks down to death.
      Her ways lead to the souls of the dead.
19         None who have sex with her
          come back.
        Nor do they ever reach the paths
          of life.

20 So walk in the way of good people
    and stay on the paths of righteous people.
21       Decent people will live in the land.
      People of integrity will remain in it.
22         But wicked people will be cut off
          from the land
          and treacherous people will be torn[a]
          from it.

---

[a] 2:22 Or "will be swept away."

# *Day 6* ⁓

## PSALM 12

For the choir director; on the *sheminith*; a psalm by David.

1   Help, O LORD.
       No godly person is left.
       Faithful people have vanished
           from among Adam's descendants!

2   All people speak foolishly.
   They speak with flattering lips.
       They say one thing but mean another.

3       May the LORD cut off every flattering lip
       and every bragging tongue

4           that has said,
               "We will overcome with our tongues.
               With lips such as ours,
                   who can be our master?"

5   "Because oppressed people are robbed
           and needy people groan,
       I will now arise," says the LORD.
       "I will provide safety for those who long for it."

6   The promises of the LORD are pure,
       like silver refined in a furnace*
           and purified seven times.

7   O LORD, you will protect them.
   You will keep each one safe
       from those people forever.

8       Wicked people parade around

---

*a* 12:6 Hebrew meaning uncertain.

when immorality increases among
Adam's descendants.


## PSALM 13

For the choir director; a psalm by David.

1   How long, O LORD? Will you forget me forever?
How long will you hide your face from me?
2   How long must I make decisions alone
with sorrow in my heart day after day?
How long will my enemy triumph over me?

3   Look at me! Answer me, O LORD my God!
Light up my eyes,
or else I will die
4       and my enemy will say,
"I have overpowered him."
My opponents will rejoice
because I have been shaken.

5   But I trust your mercy.
My heart finds joy in your salvation.
6   I will sing to the LORD
because he has been good to me.


## PSALM 14[a]

For the choir director; by David.

1   Godless fools say in their hearts,
"There is no God."

---

[a] 14:1 Psalm 14 is virtually identical in wording to Psalm 53.

They are corrupt.
They do disgusting things.
   There is no one who does good things.
2   The LORD looks down from heaven
         on Adam's descendants
      to see if there is anyone who acts wisely,
         if there is anyone who seeks help from God.
3   Everyone has turned away.
         Together they have become rotten to the core.
            No one, not even one person,
               does good things.
4   Are all those troublemakers,
         those who devour my people
            as if they were devouring food,
         so ignorant that they do not call on the LORD?
5   There they are—panic-stricken
         because God is with the person who is righteous.
6   They put the advice of oppressed people to shame
         because the LORD is their refuge.

7   If only salvation for Israel would come from Zion!
   When the LORD restores the fortunes of his people,
      Jacob will rejoice.
      Israel will be glad.


## PSALM 15

A psalm by David.

1   O LORD, who may stay in your tent?
   Who may live on your holy mountain?

2      The one who walks with integrity,
         does what is righteous,
         and speaks the truth within his heart.

**3**　The one who does not slander with his tongue,
　　　do evil to a friend,
　　　　or bring disgrace on his neighbor.

**4**　The one who despises those rejected by God
　　　but honors those who fear the LORD.

　　The one who makes a promise
　　　and does not break it,
　　　even though he is hurt by it.

**5**　The one who does not collect interest on a loan
　　　or take a bribe against an innocent person.

Whoever does these things will never be shaken.

## PROVERBS 3:1-12

### Using Wisdom

**1**　My son,
　　　do not forget my teachings,
　　　　and keep my commands in mind,
**2**　　　　because they will bring you
　　　　　long life, good years, and peace.

**3**　Do not let mercy and truth leave you.
　　Fasten them around your neck.
　　Write them on the tablet of your heart.
**4**　　Then you will find favor and much success
　　　in the sight of God and humanity.

**5**　Trust the LORD with all your heart,
　　　and do not rely on your own understanding.
**6**　In all your ways acknowledge him,
　　　and he will make your paths smooth.[a]

---

[a] 3:6 Or "straight."

7  Do not consider yourself wise.
   Fear the LORD, and turn away from evil.
8      ⌞Then⌟ your body will be healed,
          and your bones will have nourishment.

9  Honor the LORD with your wealth
      and with the first and best part
          of all your income.ᵃ
10         Then your barns will be full,
              and your vats will overflow with fresh wine.

11  Do not reject the discipline of the LORD, my son,
       and do not resent his warning,
12         because the LORD warns the one he loves,
              even as a father warns a son
                  with whom he is pleased.

# Day 7

## PSALM 16

A *miktam*ᵇ by David.

1  Protect me, O God, because I take refuge in you.
2      I said to the LORD,
          "You are my Lord.
              Without you, I have nothing good."
3  Those who lead holy lives on earth
      are the noble ones who fill me with joy.ᶜ
4  Those who quickly chase after other gods
      multiply their sorrows.

---

ᵃ 3:9 Or "harvest." ᵇ 16:1 Unknown musical term. ᶜ 16:3 English equivalent of this verse difficult.

I will not pour out
>their sacrificial offerings of blood
>or use my lips to speak their names.

5 The LORD is my inheritance and my cup.
>You are the one who determines my destiny.
6 Your boundary lines mark out
>pleasant places for me.
Indeed, my inheritance is something beautiful.

7 I will praise the LORD, who advises me.
>My conscience warns me at night.
8 I always keep the LORD in front of me.
>When he is by my side, I cannot be moved.
9 That is why my heart is glad
>and my soul rejoices.
>My body rests securely
10 because you do not abandon my soul
>to the grave
>or allow your holy one to decay.
11 You make the path of life known to me.
>Complete joy is in your presence.
>Pleasures are by your side forever.

## PSALM 17

A prayer by David.

1 Hear my plea for justice, O LORD.
>Pay attention to my cry.
>Open your ears to my prayer,
>which comes from lips free from deceit.
2 Let the verdict of my innocence
>come directly from you.
>Let your eyes observe what is fair.

3 You have probed my heart.
  You have confronted me at night.
  You have tested me like silver,
      but you found nothing wrong.
  I have determined that my mouth will not sin.
4 I have avoided cruelty because of your word.
      In spite of what others have done,
5         my steps have remained firmly in your paths.
      My feet have not slipped.
6 I have called on you because you answer me, O God.
      Turn your ear toward me.
      Hear what I have to say.
7 Reveal your miraculous deeds of mercy,
      O Savior of those who find refuge by your side
          from those who attack them.
8 Guard me as if I were the pupil in your eye.
  Hide me in the shadow of your wings.
9 Hide me from wicked people
      who violently attack me,
      from my deadly enemies who surround me.

10 They have shut out all feeling.[a]
   Their mouths have spoken arrogantly.
11 They have tracked me down.
   They have surrounded me.
   They have focused their attention on throwing me
          to the ground.
12    Each one of them is like a lion
          eager to tear its prey apart
          and like a young lion crouching in hiding places.

13 Arise, O LORD; confront them!
   Bring them to their knees!

[a] 17:10 Hebrew meaning uncertain.

With your sword rescue my life
   from wicked people.
14  With your power rescue me from mortals, O LORD,
   from mortals who enjoy their inheritance
     only in this life.
    You fill their bellies with your treasure.
     Their children are satisfied ⌞with it⌟,
      and they leave what remains
       to their children.

15  I will see your face when I am declared innocent.
   When I wake up, I will be satisfied
    ⌞with seeing⌟ you.

## PROVERBS 3:13-20

13  Blessed is the one who finds wisdom
   and the one who obtains understanding.
14    The profit ⌞gained⌟ from ⌞wisdom⌟ is greater than
     the profit ⌞gained⌟ from silver.
     Its yield is better than fine gold.
15  ⌞Wisdom⌟ is more precious than jewels,
   and all your desires cannot equal it.
16    Long life is in ⌞wisdom's⌟ right hand.
     In ⌞wisdom's⌟ left hand are riches and honor.
17  ⌞Wisdom's⌟ ways are pleasant ways,
   and all its paths lead to peace.
18  ⌞Wisdom⌟ is a tree of life
   for those who take firm hold of it.
    Those who cling to it are blessed.

19  By Wisdom the LORD laid the foundation
   of the earth.
  By understanding he established the heavens.

20   By his knowledge the deep waters were divided,
      and the skies dropped dew.

# *Day 8* ☙

## PSALM 18[a]

For the choir director; by David, the servant of the LORD.
He sang this song to the LORD when the LORD rescued
him from all his enemies, especially from Saul. He said,

1   I love you, O LORD, my strength.
2   The LORD is my rock and my fortress and my Savior,
    my God, my rock in whom I take refuge,
      my shield, and the strength of my salvation,
        my stronghold.
3   The LORD should be praised.
    I called on him, and I was saved from my enemies.

4   The ropes of death had become tangled around me.
    The torrents of destruction had overwhelmed me.
5     The ropes of the grave had surrounded me.
      The clutches of death had confronted me.

6   I called on the LORD in my distress.
    I cried to my God for help.
      He heard my voice from his temple,
        and my cry for help reached his ears.

7   Then the earth shook and quaked.
    Even the foundations of the mountains trembled.
      They shook violently because he was angry.

---

[a] 18:1 Psalm 18 is virtually identical in wording to 2 Samuel 22.

8   Smoke went up from his nostrils,
        and a raging fire came out of his mouth.
            Glowing coals flared up from it.
9   He spread apart the heavens
        and came down with a dark cloud under his feet.
10  He rode on one of the angels[a] as he flew,
        and he soared on the wings of the wind.
11  He made the darkness his hiding place,
        the dark rain clouds his covering.
12  Out of the brightness in front of him,
        those rain clouds passed by
            with hailstones and lightning.
13  The LORD thundered in the heavens.
    The Most High made his voice heard
        with hailstones and lightning.
14  He shot his arrows and scattered them.
    He flashed streaks of lightning
        and threw them into confusion.
15      Then the ocean floor could be seen.
        The foundations of the earth were laid bare
            at your stern warning, O LORD,
                at the blast of the breath from your nostrils.

16  He reached down from high above
        and took hold of me.
    He pulled me out of the raging water.
17  He rescued me from my strong enemy
        and from those who hated me,
            because they were too strong for me.
18  On the day when I faced disaster,
        they confronted me,
            but the LORD came to my defense.

---

[a] 18:10 Or "cherubim."

<sup>19</sup> He brought me out to a wide-open place.
He rescued me
because he was pleased with me.

<sup>20</sup> The Lord rewarded me
because of my righteousness,
because my hands are clean.
He paid me back
<sup>21</sup> because I have kept the ways of the Lord
and I have not wickedly turned away
from my God,
<sup>22</sup> because all his judgments are in front of me
and I have not turned away from his laws.
<sup>23</sup> I was innocent as far as he was concerned.
I have kept myself from guilt.
<sup>24</sup> The Lord paid me back
because of my righteousness,
because he can see that my hands are clean.

<sup>25</sup> ⌊In dealing⌋ with faithful people you are faithful,
with innocent people you are innocent,
<sup>26</sup> with pure people you are pure.
⌊In dealing⌋ with devious people you are clever.

<sup>27</sup> You save humble people,
but you bring down a conceited look.
<sup>28</sup> O Lord, you light my lamp.
My God turns my darkness into light.
<sup>29</sup> With you I can attack a line of soldiers.
With my God I can break through barricades.

<sup>30</sup> God's way is perfect!
The promise of the Lord has proven to be true.
He is a shield to all those
who take refuge in him.

31     Who is God but the LORD?
      Who is a rock except our God?

32  God arms me with strength
    and makes my way perfect.

33     He makes my feet like those of a deer
      and gives me sure footing on high places.

34     He trains my hands for battle
      so that my arms can bend
        an ̖archer's̗ bow of bronze.

35  You have given me the shield of your salvation.
 Your right hand supports me.
 Your gentleness makes me great.

36  You make a wide path for me to walk on
    so that my feet do not slip.

37  I chased my enemies and caught up with them.
 I did not return until I had ended their lives.

38  I wounded them so badly
    that they were unable to get up.
    They fell under my feet.

39  You armed me with strength for battle.
 You made my opponents bow at my feet.

40  You made my enemies turn their backs to me,
    and I destroyed those who hated me.

41  They cried out for help,
    but there was no one to save them.
 They cried out to the LORD,
    but he did not answer them.

42     I beat them into a powder as fine as the dust
      blown by the wind.
    I threw them out as though they were dirt
      on the streets.

43  You rescued me from my conflicts with the people.
 You made me the leader of nations.

A people I did not know will serve me:
44 As soon as they hear of me, they will obey me.
Foreigners will cringe in front of me.
45 Foreigners will lose heart,
and they will tremble
when they come out of their fortifications.

46 The LORD lives!
Thanks be to my rock!
May God my Savior be honored.
47 God gives me vengeance!
He brings people under my authority.
48 He saves me from my enemies.
You lift me up above my opponents.
You rescue me from violent people.
49 That is why I will give thanks to you,
O LORD, among the nations
and make music to praise your name.
50 He gives great victories to his king.
He shows mercy to his anointed,
to David, and to his descendant[a] forever.

## PROVERBS 3:21-28

21 My son,
do not lose sight of these things.
Use priceless wisdom and foresight.
22 Then they will mean life for you,
and they will grace your neck.
23 Then you will go safely on your way,
and you will not hurt your foot.
24 When you lie down, you will not be afraid.
As you lie there, your sleep will be sweet.

---

[a] 18:50 Or "to his descendants."

25    Do not be afraid of sudden terror
      or of the destruction of wicked people
         when it comes.
26       The LORD will be your confidence.
      He will keep your foot from getting caught.

27    Do not hold back anything good
      from those who are entitled to it
         when you have the power to do so.
28    When you have the good thing with you,
      do not tell your neighbor,
    "Go away!
    Come back tomorrow.
    I'll give you something then."

# *Day 9* ⇝

## PSALM 19

For the choir director; a psalm by David.

1    The heavens declare the glory of God,
      and the sky displays what his hands have made.
2    One day tells a story to the next.
  One night shares knowledge with the next
3       without talking,
      without words,
      without their voices being heard.
4    ⌊Yet,⌋ their sound has gone out into the entire world,
      their message to the ends of the earth.
  He has set up a tent in the heavens for the sun,
5       which comes out of its chamber like a bridegroom.
       Like a champion, it is eager to run its course.

6          It rises from one end of the heavens.
         It circles around to the other.
            Nothing is hidden from its heat.

7   The teachings of the LORD are perfect.
      They renew the soul.
  The testimony of the LORD is dependable.
      It makes gullible people wise.

8   The instructions of the LORD are correct.
      They make the heart rejoice.
  The command of the LORD is radiant.
      It makes the eyes shine.

9   The fear of the LORD is pure.
      It endures forever.
  The decisions of the LORD are true.
      They are completely fair.

10      They are more desirable than gold,
         even the finest gold.
     They are sweeter than honey,
         even the drippings from a honeycomb.

11      As your servant I am warned by them.
         There is a great reward in following them.

12   Who can notice every mistake?
      Forgive my hidden faults.

13      Keep me from sinning.
  Do not let anyone gain control over me.
      Then I will be blameless,
         and I will be free from any great offense.

14   May the words from my mouth
         and the thoughts from my heart
    be acceptable to you,
         O LORD, my rock and my defender.

## PSALM 20

For the choir director; a psalm by David.

1   The LORD will answer you in times of trouble.
    The name of the God of Jacob will protect you.
2   He will send you help from his holy place
    and support you from Zion.
3   He will remember all your grain offerings
    and look with favor on your burnt offerings.    *Selah*
4   He will give you your heart's desire
    and carry out all your plans.

5   We will joyfully sing about your victory.
    We will wave our flags in the name of our God.
    The LORD will fulfill all your requests.

6   Now I know that the LORD will give victory
      to his anointed king.
    He will answer him from his holy heaven
      with mighty deeds of his powerful hand.
7   Some ˻rely˼ on chariots and others on horses,
    but we will boast in the name of the LORD our God.
8      They will sink to their knees and fall,
      but we will rise and stand firm.

9   Give victory to the king, O LORD.
    Answer us when we call.

## PSALM 21

For the choir director; a psalm by David.

1   The king finds joy in your strength, O LORD.
    What great joy he has in your victory!
2   You gave him his heart's desire.

You did not refuse the prayer from his lips.      *Selah*

3 You welcomed him with the blessings of good things
     and set a crown of fine gold on his head.

4 He asked you for life.
     You gave him a long life, forever and ever.

5 Because of your victory his glory is great.
   You place splendor and majesty on him.

6    Yes, you made him a blessing forever.
     You made him glad with the joy of your presence.

7       Indeed, the king trusts the LORD,
          and through the mercy of the Most High,
             he will not be moved.

8 Your hand will discover all your enemies.
   Your powerful hand will find all who hate you.

9    When you appear, you will make them ⌊burn⌋
         like a blazing furnace.
      The LORD will swallow them up in his anger.
      Fire will devour them.

10 You will destroy their children from the earth
       and their offspring
           from among Adam's descendants.

11       Although they scheme and plan
              evil against you,
           they will not succeed.

12       They turn their backs ⌊and flee⌋
            because you aim your bow at their faces.*ᵃ*

13 Arise, O LORD, in your strength.
   We will sing and make music to praise your power.

---

*ᵃ* 21:12 Hebrew meaning of this verse uncertain.

## PROVERBS 3:29-35

29    Do not plan to do something wrong
          to your neighbor
       while he is sitting there with you
          and suspecting nothing.
30    Do not quarrel with a person for no reason
       if he has not harmed you.
31    Do not envy a violent person.
       Do not choose any of his ways.
32       The devious person is disgusting to the LORD.
         The LORD's intimate advice is
            with decent people.

33    The LORD curses the house of wicked people,
       but he blesses the home of righteous people.
34    When he mocks the mockers,
       he is gracious to humble people.
35    Wise people will inherit honor,
       but fools will bear disgrace.

# *Day 10* ≈

## PSALM 22

For the choir director; according to *ayyeleth hashachar;*[a]
a psalm by David.

1    My God, my God,
          why have you abandoned me?
          Why are you so far away from helping me,

---

[a] 22:1 Unknown musical term.

' so far away from the words of my groaning?
2  My God,
    I cry out by day, but you do not answer—
      also at night, but I find no rest.

3  Yet, you are holy, enthroned on the praises of Israel.
4  Our ancestors trusted you.
    They trusted, and you rescued them.
5      They cried to you and were saved.
    They trusted you and were never disappointed.

6  Yet, I am a worm and not a man.
    I am scorned by humanity and despised by people.
7  All who see me make fun of me.
    Insults pour from their mouths.
      They shake their heads and say,
8          "Put yourself in the LORD's hands.
          Let the LORD save him!
          Let God rescue him
            since he is pleased with him!"
9  Indeed, you are the one who brought me
      out of the womb,
    the one who made me feel safe
      at my mother's breasts.
10  I was placed in your care from birth.
    From my mother's womb you have been my God.

11  Do not be so far away from me.
    Trouble is near, and there is no one to help.
12      Many bulls have surrounded me.
    Strong bulls from Bashan have encircled me.
13      They have opened their mouths to attack me
      like ferocious, roaring lions.
14  I am poured out like water,

and all my bones are out of joint.
My heart is like wax.
It has melted within me.
15 My strength is dried up like pieces of broken pottery.
My tongue sticks to the roof of my mouth.
You lay me down in the dust of death.
16 Dogs have surrounded me.
A mob has encircled me.
They have pierced my hands and feet.
17     I can count all my bones.
People stare.
They gloat over me.
18     They divide my clothes among themselves.
They throw dice for my clothing.

19 Do not be so far away, O LORD.
Come quickly to help me, O my strength.
20 Rescue my soul from the sword,
my life from vicious dogs.
21 Save me from the mouth of the lion
and from the horns of wild oxen.

You have answered me.

22 I will tell my people about your name.
I will praise you within the congregation.
23 All who fear the LORD, praise him!
All you descendants of Jacob, glorify him!
Stand in awe of him, all you descendants of Israel.
24 The LORD has not despised or been disgusted
with the plight of the oppressed one.
He has not hidden his face from that person.
The LORD heard when that oppressed person
cried out to him for help.

25 My praise comes from you
while I am among those assembled for worship.
I will fulfill my vows in the presence of those
who fear the LORD.

26 Oppressed people will eat until they are full.
Those who look to the LORD will praise him.
May you live forever.

27 All the ends of the earth will remember
and return to the LORD.
All the families from all the nations will worship you

28 because the kingdom belongs to the LORD
and he rules the nations.

29 All prosperous people on earth will eat and worship.
All those who go down to the dust
will kneel in front of him,
even those who are barely alive.

30 There will be descendants who serve him,
a generation that will be told about the Lord.

31 They will tell people yet to be born
about his righteousness—
that he has finished it.

## PROVERBS 4:1-9

### Cherish Wisdom

1 Sons,
listen to ˌyourˌ father's discipline,
and pay attention in order to
gain understanding.

2 After all, I have taught you well.
Do not abandon my teachings.

3 When I was a boy ˌlearningˌ from my father,
when I was a tender and only child of my mother,

4      they used to teach me and say to me,
       "Cling to my words wholeheartedly.
       Obey my commands so that you may live.

5      Acquire wisdom.
     Acquire understanding.
     Do not forget.
     Do not turn away from the words
       that I have spoken.

6      Do not abandon wisdom,
       and it will watch over you.
     Love wisdom, and it will protect you.

7        The beginning of wisdom
         is to acquire wisdom.
     Acquire understanding with all
       that you have.

8      Cherish wisdom.
       It will raise you up.
       It will bring you honor
         when you embrace it.

9        It will give you a graceful garland
         for your head.
       It will hand you a beautiful crown."

# *Day 11* ≈

## PSALM 23

A psalm by David.

1    The LORD is my shepherd.
     I am never in need.

2        He makes me lie down in green pastures.

He leads me beside peaceful waters.

3   He renews my soul.
    He guides me along the paths of righteousness
        for the sake of his name.

4   Even though I walk
        through the dark valley of death,
    because you are with me, I fear no harm.
        Your rod and your staff give me courage.

5   You prepare a banquet for me
        while my enemies watch.
    You anoint my head with oil.
        My cup overflows.

6   Certainly, goodness and mercy will stay close to me
        all the days of my life,
    and I will remain in the LORD's house
        for days without end.

## PSALM 24

A psalm by David.

1   The earth and everything it contains are the LORD's.
    The world and all who live in it are his.

2       He laid its foundation on the seas
            and set it firmly on the rivers.

3   Who may go up the LORD's mountain?
    Who may stand in his holy place?

4       ⌊The one who⌋ has clean hands and a pure heart
            and does not long for what is false*a*
                or lie when he is under oath.

5       ⌊This person⌋ will receive a blessing from the LORD

---

*a* 24:4 Hebrew meaning uncertain.

and righteousness from God, his savior.
6   This is the person who seeks him,
        who searches for the face of the God of Jacob.[a]

                                                    *Selah*

7   Lift your heads, you gates.
    Be lifted, you ancient doors,
        so that the king of glory may come in.

8   Who is this king of glory?
        The LORD, strong and mighty!
        The LORD, heroic in battle!

9   Lift your heads, you gates.
    Be lifted, you ancient doors,
        so that the king of glory may come in.

10  Who, then, is this king of glory?
        The LORD of Armies is the king of glory!        *Selah*

## PROVERBS 4:10-19

### Stay on the Path of Wisdom

10  My son,
        listen and accept my words,
            and they will multiply the years of your life.
11          I have taught you the way of wisdom.
            I have guided you along decent paths.
12              When you walk,
                    your stride will not be hampered.
                Even if you run, you will not stumble.

13      Cling to discipline.
        Do not relax your grip on it.

---

[a] 24:6 A few Hebrew manuscripts, Greek, Syriac; Masoretic Text "your face, Jacob."

Keep it because it is your life.
14 Do not stray onto the path of wicked people.
Do not walk in the way of evil people.
15 Avoid it.
Do not walk near it.
Turn away from it,
and keep on walking.
16 Wicked people cannot sleep
unless they do wrong,
and they are robbed of their sleep
unless they make someone stumble.
17 They eat food obtained
through wrongdoing
and drink wine obtained
through violence.

18 But the path of righteous people is like
the light of dawn
that becomes brighter and brighter
until it reaches midday.
19 The way of wicked people is like deep darkness.
They do not know what makes them stumble.

# *Day 12* ≈

## PSALM 25[a]

By David.

1 To you, O LORD, I lift my soul.
2 I trust you, O my God.

---

[a] 25:1 Psalm 25 is a poem in Hebrew alphabetical order.

Do not let me be put to shame.
Do not let my enemies triumph over me.

³ No one who waits for you will ever be put to shame,
but all who are unfaithful will be put to shame.

⁴ Make your ways known to me, O LORD,
and teach me your paths.

⁵ Lead me in your truth and teach me
because you are God, my savior.
I wait all day long for you.

⁶ Remember, O LORD, your compassionate
and merciful deeds.
They have existed from eternity.

⁷ Do not remember the sins of my youth
or my rebellious ways.
Remember me, O LORD,
in keeping with your mercy
and your goodness.

⁸ The LORD is good and decent.
That is why he teaches sinners
the way they should live.

⁹ He leads humble people to do what is right,
and he teaches them his way.

¹⁰ Every path of the LORD is ⌊one of⌋ mercy and truth
for those who cling to his promise[a]
and written instructions.

¹¹ For the sake of your name, O LORD,
remove my guilt, because it is great.

¹² Who, then, is this person that fears the LORD?
He is the one whom the LORD will teach
which path to choose.

¹³ He will enjoy good things in life,

---

[a] 25:10 Or "covenant."

and his descendants will inherit the land.
14 The LORD advises those who fear him.
    He reveals to them the intent of his promise.

15 My eyes are always on the LORD.
    He removes my feet from traps.
16 Turn to me, and have pity on me.
    I am lonely and oppressed.
17 Relieve my troubled heart,
    and bring me out of my distress.
18 Look at my misery and suffering,
    and forgive all my sins.
19 See how my enemies have increased in number,
    how they have hated me with vicious hatred!
20 Protect my life, and rescue me!
Do not let me be put to shame.
    I have taken refuge in you.
21 Integrity and honesty will protect me
        because I wait for you.
22 Rescue Israel, O God, from all its troubles!


## PSALM 26

By David.

1 Judge me favorably, O LORD,
        because I have walked with integrity
            and I have trusted you without wavering.
2 Examine me, O LORD, and test me.
Look closely into my heart and mind.
3     I see your mercy in front of me.
        I walk in the light of your truth.
4     I did not sit with liars,
        and I will not be found among hypocrites.

5      I have hated the mob of evildoers
            and will not sit with wicked people.
6      I will wash my hands in innocence.
       I will walk around your altar, O LORD,
7            so that I may loudly sing
                  a hymn of thanksgiving
            and tell about all your miracles.

8      O LORD, I love the house where you live,
            the place where your glory dwells.

9      Do not sweep away my soul along
            with hardened sinners
       or my life along with bloodthirsty people.
10           Evil schemes are in their hands.
            Their right hands are full of bribes.
11     But I walk with integrity.
            Rescue me, and have pity on me.
12     My feet stand on level ground.
       I will praise the LORD with the choirs in worship.

## PROVERBS 4:20-27

### Stay Focused on Wisdom

20     My son,
            pay attention to my words.
            Open your ears to what I say.
21     Do not lose sight of these things.
       Keep them deep within your heart
22           because they are life to those who find them
                  and they heal the whole body.
23     Guard your heart more than anything else,
            because the source of your life flows from it.
24     Remove dishonesty from your mouth.

Put deceptive speech far away from your lips.
25  Let your eyes look straight ahead
    and your sight be focused in front of you.
26  Carefully walk a straight path,
    and all your ways will be secure.
27  Do not lean to the right or to the left.
Walk away from evil.

# *Day 13* &#8766;

## PSALM 27

By David.

1  The LORD is my light and my salvation.
    Who is there to fear?
The LORD is my life's fortress.
    Who is there to be afraid of?

2  Evildoers closed in on me to tear me to pieces.
    My opponents and enemies stumbled and fell.
3      Even though an army sets up camp against me,
        my heart will not be afraid.
    Even though a war breaks out against me,
        I will still have confidence ⌞in the LORD⌟.

4  I have asked one thing from the LORD.
This I will seek:
    to remain in the LORD's house
        all the days of my life
    in order to gaze at the LORD's beauty
        and to search for an answer in his temple.
5  He hides me in his shelter when there is trouble.
He keeps me hidden in his tent.

He sets me high on a rock.
6   Now my head will be raised above my enemies
          who surround me.
    I will offer sacrifices with shouts of joy in his tent.
    I will sing and make music to praise the LORD.
7   Hear, O LORD, when I cry aloud.
    Have pity on me, and answer me.
8   ₍When you said,₎
        "Seek my face,"
          my heart said to you,
              "O LORD, I will seek your face."[a]
9               Do not hide your face from me.
                Do not angrily turn me away.
          You have been my help.
                Do not leave me!
                Do not abandon me, O God, my savior!
10                  Even if my father and mother
                        abandon me,
                    the LORD will take care of me.
11  Teach me your way, O LORD.
    Lead me on a level path
        because I have enemies who spy on me.
12  Do not surrender me to the will of my opponents.
        False witnesses have risen against me.
            They breathe out violence.
13  I believe that I will see the goodness of the LORD
        in this world of the living.

14  Wait with hope for the LORD.
    Be strong, and let your heart be courageous.
    Yes, wait with hope for the LORD.

---

[a] 27:8 Hebrew meaning uncertain; Greek "My heart said to you, 'I have sought your face. O LORD, I will seek your face.' "

## PSALM 28

By David.

1 O LORD, I call to you.
  O my rock, do not turn a deaf ear to me.
    If you remain silent,
      I will be like those who go into the pit.
2 Hear my prayer for mercy when I call to you for help,
    when I lift my hands toward your most holy place.
3 Do not drag me away with wicked people,
    with troublemakers who speak of peace
        with their neighbors
      but have evil in their hearts.
4 Pay them back for what they have done,
    for their evil deeds.
  Pay them back for what their hands have done,
    and give them what they deserve.
5 The LORD will tear them down
        and never build them up again,
      because they never consider what he has done
        or what his hands have made.

6 Thank the LORD!
    He has heard my prayer for mercy!
7 The LORD is my strength and my shield.
  My heart trusted him, so I received help.
  My heart is triumphant;
      I give thanks to him with my song.

8 The LORD is the strength of his people
    and a fortress for the victory of his Messiah.[a]
9 Save your people, and bless those who belong to you.
  Be their shepherd, and carry them forever.

---

[a] 28:8 Or "anointed one."

## PROVERBS 5:1-14

### Avoid Adultery

1 My son,
>    pay attention to my wisdom.
>    Open your ears to my understanding
2 >    so that you may act with foresight
>    >    and speak with insight.

3 The lips of an adulterous woman drip with honey.
>    Her kiss is smoother than oil,
4 >    but in the end she is as bitter as wormwood,
>    >    as sharp as a two-edged sword.
5 Her feet descend to death.
>    Her steps lead straight to hell.
6 >    She doesn't even think about the path of life.
>    Her steps wander, and she doesn't realize it.

7 But now, sons,
>    listen to me,
>    >    and do not turn away from what I say to you.
8 Stay far away from her.
>    Do not even go near her door.
9 >    Either you will surrender your reputation
>    >    to others
>    and ˌthe rest ofˌ your years
>    >    to some cruel person,
10 >    or strangers will benefit from your strength
>    and you will have to work hard
>    >    in a pagan's house.
11 Then you will groan when your end comes,
>    when your body and flesh are consumed.
>    You will say,
12 >    "Oh, how I hated discipline!

How my heart despised correction!

13      I didn't listen to what my teachers said
to me,
nor did I keep my ear open
to my instructors.

14      I almost reached total ruin
in the assembly and in the congregation."

# *Day 14* ⁂

## PSALM 29

A psalm by David.

1   Give to the LORD, you heavenly beings.
Give to the LORD glory and power.

2   Give to the LORD the glory his name deserves.
Worship the LORD in ͺhisͺ holy splendor.

3   The voice of the LORD rolls over the water.
The God of glory thunders.
The LORD shouts over raging water.

4   The voice of the LORD is powerful.
The voice of the LORD is majestic.

5   The voice of the LORD breaks the cedars.
The LORD splinters the cedars of Lebanon.

6      He makes Lebanon skip along like a calf
and Mount Sirion like a wild ox.

7   The voice of the LORD strikes
with flashes of lightning.

8   The voice of the LORD makes the wilderness tremble.
The LORD makes the wilderness
of Kadesh tremble.

⁹ The voice of the LORD splits the oaks[a]
    and strips ˌthe trees ofˌ the forests bare.
      Everyone in his temple is saying, "Glory!"

¹⁰ The LORD sat enthroned over the flood.
The LORD sits enthroned as king forever.

¹¹ The LORD will give power to his people.
The LORD will bless his people with peace.

## PSALM 30

A psalm by David sung at the dedication of the temple.

¹ I will honor you highly, O LORD,
    because you have pulled me out ˌof the pitˌ
      and have not let my enemies rejoice over me.

² O LORD my God,
    I cried out to you for help,
      and you healed me.

³ O LORD, you brought me up from the grave.
    You called me back to life
      from among those who had gone into the pit.

⁴ Make music to praise the LORD,
    you faithful people who belong to him.
Remember his holiness by giving thanks.

⁵ His anger lasts only a moment.
His favor lasts a lifetime.
    Weeping may last for the night,
      but there is a song of joy in the morning.

⁶ When all was well with me, I said,
    "I will never be shaken."

⁷ O LORD, by your favor
    you have made my mountain stand firm.

---

[a] 29:9 Hebrew meaning of "splits the oaks" uncertain.

When you hid your face, I was terrified.
8  I will cry out to you, O LORD.
   I will plead to the Lord for mercy:
9      "How will you profit if my blood is shed,
          if I go into the pit?
       Will the dust ˎof my bodyˏ give thanks to you?
       Will it tell about your truth?"
10 Hear, O LORD, and have pity on me!
   O LORD, be my helper!
11 You have changed my sobbing into dancing.
   You have removed my sackcloth
       and clothed me with joy
12   so that my soul[a] may praise you
       with music and not be silent.
   O LORD my God, I will give thanks to you forever.

## PROVERBS 5:15-23

15   Drink water out of your own cistern
        and running water from your own well.
16         Why should water flow out of your spring?
           Why should your streams flow
              into the streets?
17           They should be yours alone,
                so do not share them with strangers.
18   Let your own fountain be blessed,
        and enjoy the girl you married
           when you were young,
19         a loving doe and a graceful deer.[b]
       Always let her breasts satisfy you.
       Always be intoxicated with her love.
20         Why should you, my son,

---

[a] 30:12 Or "glory."   [b] 5:19 Or "graceful goat."

be intoxicated with an adulterous woman
and fondle a loose woman's breast?

21 Each person's ways are clearly seen by the LORD,
and he surveys all his actions.
22 A wicked person will be trapped
by his own wrongs,
and he will be caught in the ropes
of his own sin.
23 He will die for his lack of discipline
and stumble around
because of his great stupidity.

# *Day 15* ≈

## PSALM 31

For the choir director; a psalm by David.

1 I have taken refuge in you, O LORD.
Never let me be put to shame.
Save me because of your righteousness.
2 Turn your ear toward me.
Rescue me quickly.
Be a rock of refuge for me,
a strong fortress to save me.
3 Indeed, you are my rock and my fortress.
For the sake of your name, lead me and guide me.
4 You are my refuge,
so pull me out of the net
that they have secretly laid for me.
5 Into your hands I entrust my spirit.

You have rescued me, O LORD,
God of truth.

⁶ I hate those who cling to false gods,
      but I trust the LORD.
⁷ I will rejoice and be glad because of your mercy.
      You have seen my misery.
      You have known the troubles in my soul.
⁸ You have not handed me over to the enemy.
      You have set my feet in a place
            where I can move freely.

⁹ Have pity on me, O LORD, because I am in distress.
      My eyes, my soul, and my body
            waste away from grief.
¹⁰ My life is exhausted from sorrow,
            my years from groaning.
      My strength staggers under the weight
            of my guilt,
      and my bones waste away.
¹¹ I have become a disgrace
            because of all my opponents.
      I have become someone dreaded by my friends,
            even by my neighbors.
            Those who see me on the street
                  run away from me.
¹² I have faded from memory as if I were dead
            and have become
                  like a piece of broken pottery.
¹³ I have heard the whispering of many people—
            terror on every side—
                  while they made plans together against me.
                  They were plotting to take my life.

14   I trust you, O LORD.
    I said, "You are my God."

15   My future is in your hands.
     Rescue me from my enemies,
      from those who persecute me.
16      Smile on me.
     Save me with your mercy.
17   O LORD, I have called on you,
     so do not let me be put to shame,
  Let wicked people be put to shame.
  Let them be silent in the grave.
18   Let ˌtheirˌ lying lips be speechless,
     since they speak against righteous people
      with arrogance and contempt.

19   Your kindness is so great!
     You reserve it for those who fear you.
      Adam's descendants watch
      as you show it to those
       who take refuge in you.
20      You hide them in the secret place
      of your presence
     from those who scheme against them.
     You keep them in a shelter,
      safe from quarrelsome tongues.
21   Thank the LORD!
     He has shown me the miracle of his mercy
      in a city under attack.
22   When I was panic-stricken, I said,
     "I have been cut off from your sight."
  But you heard my pleas for mercy
     when I cried out to you for help.
23   Love the LORD, all you godly ones!

The L ORD protects faithful people,
　　　but he pays back in full
　　　　　those who act arrogantly.
24 Be strong, all who wait with hope for the L ORD,
　　　and let your heart be courageous.

## PROVERBS 6:1-8

### Avoid Disaster

1 My son,
　　　if you guarantee a loan for your neighbor
　　　　　or pledge yourself for a stranger
　　　　　　　with a handshake,
2 　　　　　you are trapped by the words
　　　　　　　of your own mouth,
　　　　　　　　caught by your own promise.

3 　　Do the following things, my son,
　　　　　so that you may free yourself,
　　　　because you have fallen
　　　　　　into your neighbor's hands:
　　　　　　Humble yourself,
　　　　　　　and pester your neighbor.
4 　　　　Don't let your eyes rest
　　　　　　or your eyelids close.
5 　　　　Free yourself like a gazelle from the hand
　　　　　　　of a hunter
　　　　　　and like a bird from the hand of a hunter.

6 　Consider the ant, you lazy bum.
　　Watch its ways, and become wise.
7 　　Although it has no overseer, officer, or ruler,
8 　　　　in summertime it stores its food supply.
　　　　　At harvest time it gathers its food.

# *Day 16* ≈

## PSALM 32

A psalm by David; a *maskil.*[a]

¹   Blessed is the person whose disobedience is forgiven
        and whose sin is pardoned.
²   Blessed is the person whom the LORD never accuses
        of sin
        and who has no deceitful thoughts.

³   When I kept silent ⌊about my sins⌋,
        my bones began to weaken
                because of my groaning all day long.
⁴   Day and night your hand laid heavily on me.
    My strength shriveled in the summer heat.          *Selah*

⁵   I made my sins known to you,
            and I did not cover up my guilt.
    I decided to confess them to you, O LORD.
        Then you forgave all my sins.          *Selah*

⁶   For this reason let all godly people pray to you
        when you may be found.
            Then raging floodwater will not reach them.

⁷   You are my hiding place.
    You protect me from trouble.
    You surround me with joyous songs of salvation.
                                              *Selah*

---

[a] 32:1 Unknown musical term.

⁸ ⌐The Lord says,⌐
    "I will instruct you.
    I will teach you the way that you should go.
    I will advise you as my eyes watch over you.
⁹ Don't be stubborn like a horse or mule.
    ⌐They need⌐ a bit and bridle in their mouth
        to restrain them,
      or they will not come near you."

¹⁰ Many heartaches await wicked people,
      but mercy surrounds those who trust the Lord.

¹¹ Be glad and find joy in the Lord,
      you righteous people.
    Sing with joy, all whose motives are decent.


## PSALM 33

¹ Joyfully sing to the Lord, you righteous people.
      Praising ⌐the Lord⌐ is proper for decent people.
² Give thanks with a lyre to the Lord.
    Make music for him on a ten-stringed harp.
³ Sing a new song to him.
    Play beautifully and joyfully on stringed instruments.

⁴ The word of the Lord is correct,
      and everything he does is trustworthy.
⁵ The Lord loves righteousness and justice.
      His mercy fills the earth.
⁶ The heavens were made by the word of the Lord
      and all the stars by the breath of his mouth.
⁷ He gathers the water in the sea like a dam
      and puts the oceans in his storehouses.
⁸ Let all the earth fear the Lord.
    Let all who live in the world stand in awe of him.

9 He spoke, and it came into being.
   He gave the order, and there it stood.

10 The LORD blocks the plans of the nations.
   He frustrates the schemes of the people
        of the world.
11  The LORD's plan stands firm forever.
    His thoughts stand firm in every generation.
12 Blessed is the nation whose God is the LORD.
   Blessed are the people he has chosen as his own.

13 The LORD looks down from heaven.
   He sees all of Adam's descendants.
14 From the place where he sits enthroned,
       he looks down upon all who live on earth.
15 The one who formed their hearts
       understands everything they do.

16 No king achieves a victory with a large army.
   No warrior rescues himself
        by his own great strength.
17 Horses are not a guarantee for victory.
       Their great strength cannot help someone escape.
18 The LORD's eyes are on those who fear him,
       on those who wait with hope for his mercy
19        to rescue their souls from death
            and keep them alive during a famine.

20 We wait for the LORD.
   He is our help and our shield.
21  In him our hearts find joy.
    In his holy name we trust.
22 Let your mercy rest on us, O LORD,
       since we wait with hope for you.

## PROVERBS 6:9-19

9 How long will you lie there, you lazy bum?
  When will you get up from your sleep?
10  "Just a little sleep,
   just a little slumber,
   just a little nap."
11   Then your poverty will come ˌto youˌ
    like a drifter,
    and your need will come ˌto youˌ
     like a bandit.

12 A good-for-nothing scoundrel is a person
   who has a dishonest mouth.
13  He winks his eye,
   makes a signal with his foot,
    ˌandˌ points with his fingers.
14  He devises evil all the time with a twisted mind.
  He spreads conflict.
15   That is why disaster will come on him suddenly.
   In a moment he will be crushed
    beyond recovery.

16 There are six things that the LORD hates,
   even seven that are disgusting to him:
17   arrogant eyes,
   a lying tongue,
   hands that kill innocent people,
18   a mind devising wicked plans,
   feet that are quick to do wrong,
19   a dishonest witness spitting out lies,
    and a person who spreads conflict
     among relatives.

# *Day 17* ≈

## PSALM 34[a]

By David when he pretended to be insane in the
presence of Abimelech; Abimelech threw him out,
so David left.

1  I will thank the LORD at all times.
     My mouth will always praise him.
2  My soul will boast about the LORD.
     Those who are oppressed will hear it and rejoice.
3  Praise the LORD's greatness with me.
     Let us highly honor his name together.
4  I went to the LORD for help.
     He answered me and rescued me
        from all my fears.
5  All who look to him will be radiant.[b]
     Their faces will never be covered with shame.
6  Here is a poor man who called out.
     The LORD heard him and saved him
        from all his troubles.
7  The Messenger of the LORD camps
        around those who fear him,
     and he rescues them.
8  Taste and see that the LORD is good.
     Blessed is the person who takes refuge in him.

---

[a] 34:1 Psalm 34 is a poem in Hebrew alphabetical order.  [b] 34:5 Hebrew meaning uncertain.

9   Fear the LORD, you holy people who belong to him.
      Those who fear him are never in need.
10  Young lions go hungry and may starve,
      but those who seek the LORD's help
        have all the good things they need.
11  Come, children, listen to me.
      I will teach you the fear of the LORD.
12  Which of you wants a full life?
      Who would like to live long enough
        to enjoy good things?
13  Keep your tongue from saying evil things
      and your lips from speaking deceitful things.
14  Turn away from evil, and do good.
      Seek peace, and pursue it!
15  The LORD's eyes are on righteous people.
      His ears hear their cry for help.
16  The LORD confronts those who do evil
      in order to wipe out all memory of them
        from the earth.
17  Righteous people cry out.
      The LORD hears and rescues them
        from all their troubles.
18  The LORD is near to those whose hearts are humble.
      He saves those whose spirits are crushed.
19  The righteous person has many troubles,
      but the LORD rescues him from all of them.
20  The LORD guards all of his bones.
      Not one of them is broken.
21  Evil will kill wicked people,
      and those who hate righteous people
        will be condemned.
22  The LORD protects the souls of his servants.
      All who take refuge in him will never be condemned.

## PROVERBS 6:20-35

*More Advice About Avoiding Adultery*

20   My son,
> Obey the command of your father,
> > and do not disregard the teachings
> > > of your mother.

21   Fasten them on your heart forever.
Hang them around your neck.

22     When you walk around, they will lead you.
When you lie down, they will watch over you.
When you wake up, they will talk to you

23      because the command is a lamp,
> the teachings are a light,
> > and the warnings from discipline
> > are the path of life

24       to keep you from an evil woman
> > and from the smooth talk
> > > of a loose woman.

25   Do not desire her beauty in your heart.
Do not let her catch you with her eyes.

26    A prostitute's price is ⌊only⌋ a loaf of bread,
> but a married woman hunts
> > for ⌊your⌋ life itself.

27    Can a man carry fire in his lap
> without burning his clothes?

28    Can anyone walk on red-hot coals
> without burning his feet?

29   So it is with a man who has sex
> with his neighbor's wife.
> None who touch her will escape punishment.

30   People do not despise a thief who is hungry

when he steals to satisfy his appetite,
31
but when he is caught,
he has to repay it seven times.
He must give up all the possessions
in his house.

32 Whoever commits adultery with a woman
has no sense.
Whoever does this destroys himself.
33 An adulterous man will find disease[a]
and dishonor,
and his disgrace will not be blotted out,
34 because jealousy arouses a husband's fury.
The husband will show no mercy
when he takes revenge.
35 No amount of money
will change his mind.
The largest bribe will not satisfy him.

# *Day 18* &#x2733;

## PSALM 35

By David.

1 O Lord, attack those who attack me.
Fight against those who fight against me.
2 Use your shields, ˌbothˌ small and large.
Arise to help me.

---

[a] 6:33 Or "wounds."

3    Hold your spear to block the way
        of those who pursue me.
    Say to my soul, "I am your savior."

4   Let those who seek my life be put to shame
       and disgraced.
   Let those who plan my downfall
       be turned back in confusion.

5   Let them be like husks blown by the wind
       as the Messenger of the LORD chases them.

6   Let their path be dark and slippery
       as the Messenger of the LORD pursues them.

7   For no reason they hid their net in a pit.
   For no reason they dug the pit to trap me.

8   Let destruction surprise them.
       Let the net that they hid catch them.
       Let them fall into their own pit and be destroyed.

9   My soul will find joy in the LORD
       and be joyful about his salvation.

10  All my bones will say,
       "O LORD, who can compare with you?
      You rescue the weak person from the one
        who is too strong for him
      and weak and needy people from the one
        who robs them."

11  Malicious people bring charges against me.
   They ask me things I know nothing about.

12  I am devastated
       because they pay me back with evil
        instead of good.

13  But when they were sick, I wore sackcloth.
   I humbled myself with fasting.
       When my prayer returned unanswered,

<sup>14</sup>        I walked around as if I were mourning
                for my friend or my brother.
            I was bent over as if I were mourning
                for my mother.

<sup>15</sup>    Yet, when I stumbled,
            they rejoiced and gathered together.
        They gathered together against me.
            Unknown attackers tore me apart
                without stopping.
<sup>16</sup>        With crude and abusive mockers,
            they grit their teeth at me.
<sup>17</sup>    O Lord, how long will you look on?
        Rescue me from their attacks.
        Rescue my precious life from the lions.
<sup>18</sup>        I will give you thanks in a large gathering.
            I will praise you in a crowd ˌof worshipersˌ.

<sup>19</sup>    Do not let my treacherous enemies gloat over me.
    Do not let those who hate me for no reason
            winkˌat meˌ.
<sup>20</sup>        They do not talk about peace.
            Instead, they scheme
                against the peaceful people in the land.
<sup>21</sup>        They open their big mouths and say about me,
            "Aha! Aha! Our own eyes have seen it."
<sup>22</sup>    You have seen it, O LORD.
        Do not remain silent.
    O Lord, do not be so far away from me.
<sup>23</sup>        Wake up, and rise to my defense.
        Plead my case, O my God and my Lord.
<sup>24</sup>        Judge me by your righteousness, O LORD my God.
    Do not let them gloat over me
<sup>25</sup>        or think, "Aha, just what we wanted!"

Do not let them say, "We have swallowed him up."
26 Let those who gloat over my downfall
    be thoroughly put to shame and confused.
  Let those who promote themselves at my expense
    be clothed with shame and disgrace.
27 Let those who are happy
    when I am declared innocent
  joyfully sing and rejoice.
  Let them continually say, "The LORD is great.
    He is happy when his servant has peace."
28 Then my tongue will tell about your righteousness,
    about your praise all day long.


## PSALM 36

For the choir director; by David, the LORD's servant.

1 There is an inspired truth about the wicked person
    who has rebellion in the depths of his heart:
      He is not terrified of God.
2     He flatters himself and does not hate
      or ˌevenˌ recognize his guilt.
3 The words from his mouth
    are ˌnothing butˌ trouble and deception.
  He has stopped doing what is wise and good.
4     He invents trouble while lying on his bed
      and chooses to go the wrong direction.
    He does not reject evil.

5 O LORD, your mercy reaches to the heavens,
    your faithfulness to the skies.
6 Your righteousness is like the mountains of God,
    your judgments like the deep ocean.
      You save people and animals, O LORD.

7 Your mercy is so precious, O God,
   that Adam's descendants take refuge
      in the shadow of your wings.
8 They are refreshed
      with the rich foods in your house,
   and you make them drink
      from the river of your pleasure.
9 Indeed, the fountain of life is with you.
   In your light we see light.
10 Continue to show your mercy to those
      who know you
   and your righteousness to those
      whose motives are decent.
11 Do not let the feet of arrogant people step on me
   or the hands of wicked people push me away.
12      Look at the troublemakers who have fallen.
   They have been pushed down
      and are unable to stand up again.

## PROVERBS 7:1-20

1 My son,
   pay attention to my words.
   Treasure my commands that are within you.
2 Obey my commands so that you may live.
   Follow my teachings just as you protect
      the pupil of your eye.
3 Tie them on your fingers.
   Write them on the tablet of your heart.
4 Say to wisdom, "You are my sister."
   Give the name "my relative" to understanding
5      in order to guard yourself
         from an adulterous woman,
            from a loose woman with her smooth talk.

6 From a window in my house I looked
     through my screen.
7 I was looking at gullible people
     when I saw a young man without much sense
       among youths.
8 He was crossing a street near her corner
     and walking toward her house
9      in the twilight,
      in the evening,
      in the dark hours of the night.

10 A woman with an ulterior motive meets him.
     She is dressed as a prostitute.
11 She is loud and rebellious.
     Her feet will not stay at home.
12      One moment she is out on the street,
      the next she is at the curb,
       on the prowl at every corner.
13 She grabs him and kisses him
     and brazenly says to him,
14 "I have some sacrificial meat.
     Today I kept my vows.
15 That's why I came to meet you.
     Eagerly, I looked for you,
      and I've found you.
16 I've made my bed,
     with colored sheets of Egyptian linen.
17 I've sprinkled my bed with myrrh, aloes,
     and cinnamon.
18 Come, let's drink our fill of love until morning.
     Let's enjoy making love,
19      because my husband's not home.
      He has gone on a long trip.

20     He took lots of money with him.
       He won't be home for a couple of weeks."

# *Day 19* ❦

## PSALM 37[a]

By David.

1   Do not be preoccupied with evildoers.
    Do not envy those who do wicked things.
2       They will quickly dry up like grass
            and wither away like green plants.
3   Trust the LORD, and do good things.
    Live in the land, and practice being faithful.
4   Be happy with the LORD,
        and he will give you the desires of your heart.
5   Entrust your ways to the LORD.
    Trust him, and he will act ˌon your behalfˌ.
6       He will make your righteousness shine like a light,
            your just cause like the noonday sun.
7   Surrender yourself to the LORD,
        and wait patiently for him.
    Do not be preoccupied with ˌan evildoerˌ
            who succeeds in his way
            when he carries out his schemes.
8   Let go of anger, and leave rage behind.
        Do not be preoccupied.
            It only leads to evil.
9   Evildoers will be cut off ˌfrom their inheritanceˌ,

---

[a] 37:1 Psalm 37 is a poem in Hebrew alphabetical order.

but those who wait with hope for the LORD
will inherit the land.

10 In a little while a wicked person will vanish.
Then you can carefully examine where he was,
but there will be no trace of him.
11 Oppressed people will inherit the land
and will enjoy unlimited peace.
12 The wicked person plots against a righteous one
and grits his teeth at him.
13 The Lord laughs at him
because he has seen that his time is coming.
14 Wicked people pull out their swords
and bend their bows
to kill oppressed and needy people,
to slaughter those who are decent.
15 ˌButˌ their own swords will pierce their hearts,
and their bows will be broken.
16 The little that the righteous person has is better
than the wealth of many wicked people.
17 The arms of wicked people will be broken,
but the LORD continues
to support righteous people.
18 The LORD knows the daily ˌstrugglesˌ
of innocent people.
Their inheritance will last forever.
19 They will not be put to shame in trying times.
Even in times of famine they will be satisfied.
20 But wicked people will disappear.
The LORD's enemies will vanish
like the best part of a meadow.
They will vanish like smoke.
21 A wicked person borrows, but he does not repay.

A righteous person is generous and giving.

<sup>22</sup> Those who are blessed by him
will inherit the land.
Those who are cursed by him will be cut off.

<sup>23</sup> A person's steps are directed by the LORD,
and the LORD delights in his way.
<sup>24</sup> When he falls, he will not be thrown down headfirst
because the LORD holds on to his hand.
<sup>25</sup> I have been young, and now I am old,
but I have never seen a righteous person abandoned
or his descendants begging for food.
<sup>26</sup> He is always generous and lends freely.
His descendants are a blessing.
<sup>27</sup> Avoid evil, do good, and live forever.
<sup>28</sup> The LORD loves justice,
and he will not abandon his godly ones.
They will be kept safe forever,
but the descendants of wicked people
will be cut off.
<sup>29</sup> Righteous people will inherit the land
and live there permanently.
<sup>30</sup> The mouth of the righteous person
reflects on wisdom.
His tongue speaks what is fair.
<sup>31</sup> The teachings of his God are in his heart.
His feet do not slip.
<sup>32</sup> The wicked person watches the righteous person
and seeks to kill him.
<sup>33</sup> But the LORD will not abandon him
to the wicked person's power
or condemn him when he is brought to trial.
<sup>34</sup> Wait with hope for the LORD, and follow his path,

and he will honor you by giving you the land.
  When wicked people are cut off, you will see it.

35  I have seen a wicked person ˌacting likeˌ a tyrant,
     spreading himself out like a large cedar tree.
36  But he moved on, and now there is no trace of him.
     I searched for him, but he could not be found.
37  Notice the innocent person,
     and look at the decent person,
       because the peacemaker has a future.
38        But rebels will be completely destroyed.
           The future of wicked people will be cut off.
39  The victory for righteous people
       comes from the LORD.
     He is their fortress in times of trouble.
40  The LORD helps them and rescues them.
   He rescues them from wicked people.
   He saves them because they have taken refuge
     in him.

## PROVERBS 7:21-27

21  With all her seductive charms, she persuades him.
   With her smooth lips, she makes him give in.
22        He immediately follows her
           like a steer on its way to be slaughtered,
           like a ram hobbling into captivity[a]
23            until an arrow pierces his heart,
             like a bird darting into a trap.
           He does not realize that it will cost him his life.

24  Now, sons,
     listen to me.

---

[a] 7:22 Hebrew meaning of this line uncertain.

Pay attention to the words from my mouth.
25  Do not let your heart be turned to her ways.
Do not wander onto her paths,
26  because she has brought down many victims,
and she has killed all too many.
27  Her home is the way to hell
and leads to the darkest vaults of death.

# *Day 20* &#10158;

## PSALM 38

A psalm by David; to be kept in mind.[a]

1  O LORD, do not angrily punish me
or discipline me in your wrath.
2  Your arrows have struck me.
Your hand has struck me hard.
3  No healthy spot is left on my body
because of your rage.
There is no peace in my bones
because of my sin.

4  My guilt has overwhelmed me.
Like a heavy load, it is more than I can bear.
5  My wounds smell rotten.
They fester because of my stupidity.
6  I am bent over and bowed down very low.

---

[a] 38:1 Hebrew meaning of "to be kept in mind" uncertain.

All day I walk around in mourning.
7   My insides are filled with burning pain,
and no healthy spot is left on my body.
8   I am numb and completely devastated.
I roar because my heart's in turmoil.
.9  You know all my desires, O Lord,
and my groaning has not been hidden from you.
10  My heart is pounding.
I have lost my strength.
Even the light of my eyes has left me.

11  My loved ones and my friends keep their distance
and my relatives stand far away
because of my sickness.
12  Those who seek my life lay traps for me.
Those who are out to harm me
talk about ruining me.
All day long they think of ways to deceive me.
13  But I am like a person who cannot hear
and like a person who cannot speak.
14  I am like one who cannot hear
and who can offer no arguments.

15  But I wait with hope for you, O Lord.
You will answer, O Lord, my God.
16  I said, "Do not let them gloat over me.
When my foot slips,
do not let them promote themselves
at my expense."
17  I am ready to fall.
I am continually aware of my pain.
18  I confess my guilt.
My sin troubles me.

19    My mortal enemies are growing stronger.
          Many hate me for no reason.
20    They pay me back with evil instead of good,
          and they accuse me
                because I try to do what is good.

21    Do not abandon me, O LORD.
      O my God, do not be so distant from me.
22    Come quickly to help me, O Lord, my savior.


## PSALM 39

For the choir director; for Jeduthun; a psalm by David.

1     I said,
          "I will watch my ways so that I do not sin
                with my tongue.
          I will bridle my mouth while wicked people
                are in my presence."
2     I remained totally speechless.
      I kept silent, although it did me no good.
          While I was deep in thought, my pain grew worse.
3             My heart burned like a fire flaring up within me.
      Then I spoke with my tongue:
4             "Teach me, O LORD, about the end of my life.
          Teach me about the number of days I have left
                so that I may know how temporary my life is.
5             Indeed, you have made the length of my days
                      ⸤only⸥ a few inches.
          My life span is nothing compared to yours.
          Certainly, everyone alive
                is like a whisper in the wind.          *Selah*
6             Each person who walks around is like a shadow.
          They are busy for no reason.

They accumulate riches without knowing
who will get them."

7   And now, Lord, what am I waiting for?
    My hope is in you!
8   Rescue me from all my rebellious acts.
    Do not disgrace me in front of godless fools.
9   I remained speechless.
    I did not open my mouth
        because you are the one who has done this.
10  Remove the sickness you laid upon me.
        My life is over because you struck me
            with your hand.
11  With stern warnings you discipline people
        for their crimes.
    Like a moth you eat away at what is dear to them.
    Certainly, everyone is like a whisper in the wind. *Selah*

12  Listen to my prayer, O LORD.
    Open your ear to my cry for help.
    Do not be deaf to my tears,
        for I am a foreign resident with you,
            a stranger like all my ancestors.
13  Look away from me so that I may smile again
        before I go away and am no more.

## PROVERBS 8:1-11

### Wisdom's Announcement

1   Does not wisdom call out?
    Does not understanding raise its voice?
2   ⌊Wisdom⌋ takes its stand on high ground,
        by the wayside where the roads meet,
3       near the gates to the city.

At the entrance ⸤wisdom⸣ sings its song,

**4**      "I am calling to all of you,
and my appeal is to all people.

**5**          You gullible people,
learn how to be sensible.
You fools, get a heart
that has understanding.[a]

**6**      Listen! I am speaking about noble things,
and my lips will say what is right.

**7**      My mouth expresses the truth,
and wickedness is disgusting to my lips.

**8**      Everything I say is fair,
and there is nothing twisted or crooked in it.

**9**          All of it is clear to a person
who has understanding
and right to those
who have acquired knowledge.

**10**      Take my discipline, not silver,
and my knowledge rather than fine gold,

**11**          because wisdom is better than jewels.
Nothing you desire can equal it.

# *Day 21* ❧

## PSALM 40

For the choir director; a psalm by David.

**1**      I waited patiently for the LORD.
He turned to me and heard my cry for help.

---

[a] 8:5 English equivalent difficult.

2      He pulled me out of a horrible pit,
          out of the mud and clay.
      He set my feet on a rock
          and made my steps secure.

3      He placed a new song in my mouth,
          a song of praise to our God.
          Many will see this and worship.
          They will trust the LORD.

4   Blessed is the person
      who places his confidence in the LORD
         and does not rely on arrogant people
         or those who follow lies.

5   You have done many miraculous things,
      O LORD my God.
   You have made many wonderful plans for us.
      No one compares to you!
   I will tell others about your miracles,
      which are more than I can count.

6   You were not pleased with sacrifices and offerings.
   You have dug out two ears for me.[a]
   You did not ask for burnt offerings
      or sacrifices for sin.

7      Then I said, "I have come!
         (It is written about me in the scroll of the book.)

8      I am happy to do your will, O my God."
   Your teachings are deep within me.

9   I will announce the good news of righteousness
      among those assembled for worship.
         I will not close my lips.
           You know that, O LORD.

---

[a] 40:6 Hebrew meaning of this line uncertain.

10   I have not buried your righteousness
        deep in my heart.
   I have been outspoken about your faithfulness
        and your salvation.
   I have not hidden your mercy and your truth
        from those assembled for worship.

11   Do not withhold your compassion from me, O LORD.
   May your mercy and your truth always protect me.
12      Countless evils have surrounded me.
        My sins have caught up with me
          so that I can no longer see.
        They outnumber the hairs on my head.
        I have lost heart.

13   O LORD, please rescue me!
   Come quickly to help me, O LORD![a]
14   Let all those who seek to end my life
        be confused and put to shame.
   Let those who want my downfall
        be turned back and disgraced.
15   Let those who say to me, "Aha! Aha!"
        be stunned by their own shame.
16   Let all who seek you rejoice
        and be glad because of you.
   Let those who love your salvation continually say,
        "The LORD is great!"

17   But I am oppressed and needy.
   May the Lord think of me.
      You are my help and my savior.
        O my God, do not delay!

---

[a] 40:13 Verses 13-17 are virtually identical in wording to Psalm 70.

## PSALM 41

For the choir director; a psalm by David.

1  Blessed is the one who has concern
      for helpless people.
    The LORD will rescue him in times of trouble.
2  The LORD will protect him and keep him alive.
    He will be blessed in the land.
      Do not place him at the mercy
        of his enemies.
3  The LORD will support him on his sickbed.
    You will restore this person to health
      when he is ill.

4  I said, "O LORD, have pity on me!
    Heal my soul because I have sinned against you."
5  My enemies say terrible things about me:
    "When will he die,
      and when will his family name disappear?"
6  When one of them comes to visit me,
    he speaks foolishly.
    His heart collects gossip.
      Then he leaves to tell others.
7  Everyone who hates me whispers about me.
    They think evil things about me and say,
8    "A devilish disease has attached itself to him.
    He will never leave his sickbed."
9  Even my closest friend whom I trusted,
    the one who ate my bread,
      has lifted his heel against me.
10  Have pity on me, O LORD!
    Raise me up so that I can pay them back
11    and my enemy cannot shout in triumph over me.

When you do this,
I know that you are pleased with me.
12 You defend my integrity,
and you set me in your presence forever.

13 Thank the LORD God of Israel
through all eternity!
Amen and amen!

## PROVERBS 8:12-21

### Wisdom's Authority

12 "I, Wisdom, live with insight,
and I acquire knowledge and foresight.
13 To fear the LORD is to hate evil.
I hate pride, arrogance, evil behavior,
and twisted speech.
14 Advice and priceless wisdom are mine.
I, Understanding, have strength.
15 Through me kings reign,
and rulers decree fair laws.
16 Through me princes rule,
so do nobles and all fair judges.
17 I love those who love me.
Those eagerly looking for me will find me.
18 I have riches and honor,
lasting wealth and righteousness.
19 What I produce is better than gold, pure gold.
What I yield is better than fine silver.
20 I walk in the way of righteousness,
on the paths of justice,
21 to give an inheritance to those who love me
and to fill their treasuries.

# Day 22 ≈

## PSALM 42

For the choir director; a *maskil*[a] by Korah's descendants.

1    As a deer longs for flowing streams,
        so my soul longs for you, O God.
2    My soul thirsts for God, for the living God.
        When may I come to see God's face?
3    My tears are my food day and night.
        People ask me all day long, "Where is your God?"
4    I will remember these things as I pour out my soul:
        how I used to walk with the crowd
            and lead it in a procession to God's house.
        ⌊I sang⌋ songs of joy and thanksgiving
            while crowds of people
                celebrated a festival.

5            Why are you discouraged, my soul?
            Why are you so restless?
                Put your hope in God,
                    because I will still praise him.
                        He is my savior and my God.

6    My soul is discouraged.
        That is why I will remember you
            in the land of Jordan, on the peaks of Hermon,
                on Mount Mizar.
7        One deep sea calls to another at the roar
            of your waterspouts.

---

[a] 42:1 Unknown musical term.

All the whitecaps on your waves
    have swept over me.[a]

8 The LORD commands his mercy during the day,
    and at night his song is with me—
        a prayer to the God of my life.

9     I will ask God, my rock,
        "Why have you forgotten me?
        Why must I walk around in mourning
            while the enemy oppresses me?"

10     With a shattering blow to my bones,
        my enemies taunt me.
        They ask me all day long,
            "Where is your God?"

11     Why are you discouraged, my soul?
    Why are you so restless?
        Put your hope in God,
        because I will still praise him.
        He is my savior and my God.

## PSALM 43

1 Judge me, O God,
    and plead my case against an ungodly nation.
Rescue me from deceitful and unjust people.

2     You are my fortress, O God!
        Why have you rejected me?
        Why must I walk around in mourning
            while the enemy oppresses me?

3 Send your light and your truth.
    Let them guide me.
    Let them bring me to your holy mountain
        and to your dwelling place.

---

[a] 42:7 Hebrew meaning of this verse uncertain.

4      Then let me go to the altar of God,
            to God my highest joy,
        and I will give thanks to you on the lyre,
            O God, my God.

5      Why are you discouraged, my soul?
        Why are you so restless?
           Put your hope in God,
              because I will still praise him.
                He is my savior and my God.

## PROVERBS 8:22-31

### Wisdom as Creator

22     "The LORD already possessed me long ago,
         when his way began,
           before any of his works.
23     I was appointed from everlasting
         from the first,
           before the earth began.
24     I was born
         before there were oceans
         before there were springs filled with water.
25     I was born
         before the mountains were settled
           in their places
         and before the hills,
26         when he had not yet made land or fields
         or the first dust of the world.

27        "When he set up the heavens, I was there.
        When he traced the horizon on the surface
           of the ocean,
28         when he established the skies above,

29 when he determined the currents in the ocean,
when he set a limit for the sea
so the waters would not overstep
his command,
when he traced the foundations of the earth,
30 I was beside him as a master craftsman.[a]
I made him happy day after day,
I rejoiced in front of him all the time,
31 found joy in his inhabited world,
and delighted in the human race.


# *Day 23* ❧

## PSALM 44

For the choir director; a *maskil* by Korah's descendants.

1 O God,
we have heard it with our own ears.
Our ancestors have told us
about the miracle you performed in their day,
in days long ago.
2 By your power you forced nations ˌout of the landˌ,
but you planted our ancestors ˌthereˌ.
You shattered many groups of people,
but you set our ancestors free.[b]
3 It was not with their swords
that they took possession of the land.
They did not gain victory with their own strength.

---

[a] 8:30 Hebrew meaning of "master craftsman" uncertain.   [b] 44:2 Or "and you sent them away."

It was your right hand, your arm,
>    and the light of your presence ‚that did it‚,
>        because you were pleased with them.

⁴ You alone are my king, O God.
You won those victories for Jacob.
⁵    With you we can walk over our enemies.
>    With your name we can trample
>        those who attack us.
⁶        I do not rely on my bow,
>            and my sword will never save me.
⁷ But you saved us from our enemies.
You put to shame those who hate us.
⁸ All day long we praise our God.
>    We give thanks to you forever.                    *Selah*

⁹ But now you have rejected and disgraced us.
>    You do not even go along with our armies.
¹⁰    You make us retreat from the enemy.
>        Those who hate us rob us at will.
¹¹    You hand us over to be butchered like sheep
>        and scatter us among the nations.
¹²    You sell your people for almost nothing,
>        and at that price you have gained nothing.
¹³    You made us a disgrace to our neighbors
>        and an object of ridicule and contempt
>            to those around us.
¹⁴    You made our ‚defeat‚ a proverb
>            among the nations
>        so that people shake their heads at us.
¹⁵ All day long my disgrace is in front of me.
>    Shame covers my face
¹⁶        because of the words of those who insult
>            and slander us,

because of the presence of the enemy
and the avenger.

17 Although all of this happened to us,
we never forgot you.
We never ignored your promise.*a*

18 Our hearts never turned away.
Our feet never left your path.

19 Yet, you crushed us in a place for jackals
and covered us with the shadow of death.

20 If we forgot the name of our God
or stretched out our hands to pray to another god,

21 wouldn't God find out,
since he knows the secrets in our hearts?

22 Indeed, we are being killed all day long
because of you.
We are thought of as sheep to be slaughtered.

23 Wake up! Why are you sleeping, O Lord?
Awake! Do not reject us forever!

24 Why do you hide your face?
Why do you forget our suffering and misery?

25 Our souls are bowing in the dust.
Our bodies cling to the ground.

26 Arise! Help us!
Rescue us because of your mercy!

## PROVERBS 8:32-36

### Wisdom as Lifegiver

32 "Now, sons, listen to me.
Blessed are those who follow my ways.

---

*a* 44:17 Or "covenant."

33      Listen to discipline, and become wise.
       Do not leave my ways.
34      Blessed is the person who listens to me,
       watches at my door day after day,
       waits by my doorposts.
35      Whoever finds me finds life
       and obtains favor from the LORD.
36      Whoever sins against me harms himself.
       All those who hate me love death."

# *Day 24* ᚛

## PSALM 45

For the choir director; according to *shoshannim;*[a]
a *maskil* by Korah's descendants; a love song.

1    My heart is overflowing with good news.
     I will direct my song to the king.
     My tongue is a pen for a skillful writer.

2    You are the most handsome of Adam's descendants.
     Grace is poured on your lips.
       That is why God has blessed you forever.
3    O warrior, strap your sword to your side
     with your splendor and majesty.
4    Ride on victoriously in your majesty

---

[a] 45:1 Unknown musical term.

for the cause of truth, humility, and righteousness.
Let your right hand teach you awe-inspiring things.

5   Your arrows are sharp in the heart
        of the king's enemies.
     Nations fall beneath you.

6   Your throne, O God, is forever and ever.
     The scepter in your kingdom is a scepter for justice.

7   You have loved what is right and hated what is wrong.
        That is why God, your God, has anointed you,
            rather than your companions,
                with the oil of joy.

8   All your robes are ˌfragrantˌ with myrrh,
        aloes, and cassia.
     From ivory palaces
        the music of stringed instruments delights you.

9   The daughters of kings are among your noble ladies.
     The queen takes her place at your right hand
        and wears gold from Ophir.

10  Listen, daughter! Look closely!
     Turn your earˌtoward meˌ.
     Forget your people, and forget your father's house.

11      The king longs for your beauty.
            He is your Lord.
                Worship him.

12  The people of Tyre, the richest people,
        want to win your favor with a gift.

13  The daughter of the king is glorious
        inside ˌthe palaceˌ.
     Her dress is embroidered with gold.

14  Wearing a colorful gown, she is brought to the king.
     Her bridesmaids follow her.
        They will be brought to you.

15     With joy and delight they are brought in.
        They enter the palace of the king.

16   Your sons will take the place of your father.
     You will make them princes over the whole earth.

17   I will cause your name to be remembered
        throughout every generation.
     That is why the nations will give thanks
        to you forever and ever.

## PSALM 46

For the choir director; a song by the descendants of
Korah; according to *alamoth*.[a]

1    God is our refuge and strength,
     an ever-present help in times of trouble.

2    That is why we are not afraid
     even when the earth quakes
       or the mountains topple
         into the depths of the sea.

3         Water roars and foams,
       and mountains shake
         at the surging waves.         *Selah*

4    There is a river
     whose streams bring joy to the city of God,
       the holy place where the Most High lives.

5    God is in that city.
     It cannot fall.
       God will help it at the break of dawn.

6    Nations are in turmoil, and kingdoms topple.
     The earth melts at the sound of ˻God's˼ voice.

---

[a] 46:1 Unknown musical term.

7 The LORD of Armies is with us.
   The God of Jacob is our stronghold.                    *Selah*

8 Come, see the works of the LORD,
      the devastation he has brought to the earth.
9        He puts an end to wars all over the earth.
            He breaks an archer's bow.
            He cuts spears in two.
            He burns chariots.
10 Let go ⌊of your concerns⌋!
      Then you will know that I am God.
         I rule the nations.
         I rule the earth.

11 The LORD of Armies is with us.
   The God of Jacob is our stronghold.                    *Selah*


### PROVERBS 9:1-9

*Wisdom Hosts a Banquet*

1 Wisdom has built her house.
   She has carved out her seven pillars.
2 She has prepared her meat.
   She has mixed her wine.
   She has set her table.
3 She has sent out her servant girls.
   She calls from the highest places in the city,
4    "Whoever is gullible turn in here!"

   She says to a person without sense,
5    "Come, eat my bread,
         and drink the wine I have mixed.
6    Stop being gullible and live.
      Start traveling the road to understanding."

### Wisdom Prolongs Life

7   Whoever corrects a mocker receives abuse.
    Whoever warns a wicked person gets hurt.
8       Do not warn a mocker, or he will hate you.
        Warn a wise person, and he will love you.
9           Give ⸤advice⸥ to a wise person,
                and he will become even wiser.
            Teach a righteous person,
                and he will learn more.

# Day 25 ❧

## PSALM 47

For the choir director; a psalm by Korah's descendants.

1   Clap your hands, all you people.
    Shout to God with a loud, joyful song.
2   We must fear the LORD, the Most High.
        He is the great king of the whole earth.
3       He brings people under our authority
            and ⸤puts⸥ nations under our feet.
4       He chooses our inheritance for us,
            the pride of Jacob, whom he loved.        *Selah*

5   God has gone up with a joyful shout.
    The LORD has gone up with the sound
        of a ram's horn.
6       Make music to praise God.
            Play music for him!
        Make music to praise our king.
            Play music for him!

7 God is the king of the whole earth.
　Make your best music for him!
8 God rules the nations.
　He sits upon his holy throne.

9 The influential people from the nations
　　gather together
　　as the people of the God of Abraham.
　The rulers of the earth belong to God.
　　He rules everything.


## PSALM 48

A song; a psalm by Korah's descendants.

1 The LORD is great.
　He should be highly praised.
　　His holy mountain is in the city of our God.
2 　　Its beautiful peak is the joy of the whole earth.
　Mount Zion is on the northern ridge.
　　It is the city of the great king.
3 God is in its palaces.
　He has proved that he is a stronghold.

4 The kings have gathered.
　　They marched together.
5 　　⌞When⌟ they saw ⌞Mount Zion⌟,
　　　they were astonished.
　　　They were terrified and ran away in fear.
6 　　　Trembling seized them
　　　　like the trembling
　　　　　　that a woman experiences during labor.
7 　With the east wind you smash the ships
　　of Tarshish.

8    The things we had only heard about,
           we have now seen
        in the city of the LORD of Armies,
        in the city of our God.
           God makes Zion stand firm forever.          *Selah*
9    Inside your temple
           we carefully reflect on your mercy,
           O God.
10   Like your name, O God,
           your praise ‚reaches‚ to the ends of the earth.
        Your right hand is filled with righteousness.
11   Let Mount Zion be glad
           and the cities of Judah rejoice
              because of your judgments.

12   Walk around Zion.
           Go around it.
              Count its towers.
13                Examine its embankments.
                    Walk through its palaces.
        Then you can tell the next generation,
14         "This God is our God forever and ever.
              He will lead us beyond death."


## PROVERBS 9:10-18

10   The fear of the LORD is the beginning of wisdom.
        The knowledge of the Holy One is understanding.

11   You will live longer because of me,
           and years will be added to your life.
12   If you are wise, your wisdom will help you.
        If you mock, you alone will be held responsible.

### Stupidity Imitates Wisdom's Banquet

¹³ The woman Stupidity is loud, gullible, and ignorant.[a]
¹⁴ She sits at the doorway of her house.
She is enthroned on the high ground of the city
¹⁵     and calls to those who pass by,
those minding their own business,
¹⁶         "Whoever is gullible turn in here!"

She says to a person without sense,
¹⁷     "Stolen waters are sweet,
and food eaten in secret is tasty."
¹⁸ But he does not know
that the souls of the dead are there,
that her guests are in the depths of hell.

# *Day 26* ❧

## PSALM 49

For the choir director; a psalm by Korah's descendants.

¹ Listen to this, all you people.
Open your ears, all who live in the world—
²     common people and important ones,
rich people and poor ones.
³ My mouth will speak wise sayings,
the insights I have carefully considered.
⁴ I will turn my attention to a proverb.
I will explain my riddle with the ˌmusic ofˌ a lyre.
⁵     Why should I be afraid in times of trouble,

---

[a] 9:13 Hebrew meaning of this verse uncertain.

when slanderers surround me with evil?
6        They trust their riches
                and brag about their abundant wealth.

7    No one can ever buy back another person
        or pay God a ransom for his life.
8        The price to be paid for his soul is too costly.
            He must always give up
9                in order to live forever
                    and never see the pit.

10   Indeed, one can see that wise people die,
        that foolish and stupid people
            meet the same end.
        They leave their riches to others.
11   Although they named their lands after themselves,
        their graves[a] have become their homes
            for ages to come,
        their dwelling places
            throughout every generation.

12   But mortals will not continue here
        with what they treasure.
        They are like animals that die.

13   This is the final outcome for fools and their followers
        who are delighted by what they say:            *Selah*
14       Like sheep, they are driven to hell
            with death as their shepherd.
                (Decent people will rule them
                    in the morning.)
        Their forms will decay in the grave,
            far away from their comfortable homes.

---

[a] 49:11 Greek, Syriac, Targum; Masoretic Text "their insides."

<sup>15</sup> But God will buy me back from the power of hell
because he will take me.    *Selah*
<sup>16</sup> Do not be afraid when someone becomes rich,
when the greatness of his house increases.
<sup>17</sup> He will not take anything with him
when he dies.
His greatness cannot follow him.
<sup>18</sup> Even though he blesses himself while he is alive
(and they praise you when you do well for yourself),
<sup>19</sup> he must join the generation of his ancestors,
who will never see light ⌞again⌟.

<sup>20</sup> Mortals, with what they treasure,
still don't have understanding.
They are like animals that die.


## PROVERBS 10:1-7

<sup>1</sup> The proverbs of Solomon:

### A Wise Son Is Righteous

A wise son makes his father happy,
but a foolish son brings grief to his mother.

<sup>2</sup> Treasures gained dishonestly profit no one,
but righteousness rescues from death.
<sup>3</sup> The LORD will not allow a righteous person to starve,
but he intentionally ignores the desires
of a wicked person.

<sup>4</sup> Lazy hands bring poverty,
but hard-working hands bring riches.
<sup>5</sup> Whoever gathers in the summer is a wise son.
Whoever sleeps at harvest time brings shame.

<sup>6</sup> Blessings cover the head of a righteous person,
    but violence covers the mouths of wicked people.

<sup>7</sup> The name of a righteous person remains blessed,
    but the names of wicked people will rot away.

# *Day 27* ≈

## PSALM 50

A psalm by Asaph.

<sup>1</sup> The LORD, the only true God, has spoken.
    He has summoned the earth
        from where the sun rises to where it sets.
<sup>2</sup> God shines from Zion,
    the perfection of beauty.
<sup>3</sup> Our God will come and will not remain silent.
    A devouring fire is in front of him
        and a raging storm around him.
<sup>4</sup> He summons heaven and earth to judge his people:
<sup>5</sup>     "Gather around me, my godly people
        who have made a pledge to me
            through sacrifices."

<sup>6</sup> The heavens announce his righteousness
    because God is the judge.         *Selah*

<sup>7</sup> "Listen, my people, and I will speak.
Listen, Israel, and I will testify against you:
    I am God, your God!
<sup>8</sup> I am not criticizing you for your sacrifices
    or burnt offerings,

which are always in front of me.

9 But, I will not accept another, young bull
    from your household
    or a single male goat from your pens.

10 Every creature in the forest,
    even, the cattle on a thousand hills, is mine.

11 I know every bird in the mountains.
    Everything that moves in the fields is mine.

12 If I were hungry, I would not tell you,
    because the world and all that it contains
        are mine.

13 Do I eat the meat of bulls
    or drink the blood of goats?

14 Bring your, thanks to God as a sacrifice,
    and keep your vows to the Most High.

15      Call on me in times of trouble.
        I will rescue you, and you will honor me."

16 But God says to wicked people,
    "How dare you quote my decrees
    and mouth my promises![a]

17 You hate discipline.
    You toss my words behind you.

18      When you see a thief,
            you want to make friends with him.
        You keep company with people
            who commit adultery.

19      You let your mouth say anything evil.
        Your tongue plans deceit.

20      You sit and talk against your own brother.
        You slander your own mother's son.

21      When you did these things, I remained silent.

---

[a] 50:16 Or "covenant."

That made you think I was like you.
    I will argue my point with you
       and lay it all out for you to see.
22 Consider this, you people who forget God.
    Otherwise, I will tear you to pieces,
       and there will be no one left to rescue you.
23 Whoever offers thanks as a sacrifice honors me.
    I will let everyone who continues in my way
       see the salvation that comes from God."

## PROVERBS 10:8-23

### Proverbs Concerning the Mouth

8 The one who is truly wise accepts commands,
    but the one who talks foolishly
      will be thrown down headfirst.
9 Whoever lives honestly will live securely,
    but whoever lives dishonestly will be found out.
10 Whoever winks with his eye causes heartache.
    The one who talks foolishly
      will be thrown down headfirst.
11 The mouth of a righteous person is a fountain
      of life,
    but the mouths of wicked people
      conceal violence.
12 Hate starts quarrels,
    but love covers every wrong.

13 Wisdom is found on the lips of a person
      who has understanding,
    but a rod is for the back of one without sense.
14 Those who are wise store up knowledge,
    but the mouth of a stubborn fool invites ruin.

15 The rich person's wealth is ⸌his⸍ strong city.
    Poverty ruins the poor.
16     A righteous person's reward is life.
      A wicked person's harvest is sin.
17 Whoever practices discipline is on the way to life,
    but whoever ignores a warning strays.

18 Whoever conceals hatred has lying lips.
    Whoever spreads slander is a fool.
19     Sin is unavoidable when there is much talk,
      but whoever seals his lips is wise.
20 The tongue of a righteous person is pure silver.
    The hearts of wicked people are worthless.
21 The lips of a righteous person feed many,
    but stubborn fools die
        because they have no sense.

22 It is the LORD's blessing that makes a person rich,
    and hard work adds nothing to it.
23 Like the laughter of a fool when he carries out
      an evil plan,
    so is wisdom to a person who has understanding.

# *Day 28* &#126;

## PSALM 51

For the choir director; a psalm by David when the prophet Nathan came to him after David's adultery with Bathsheba.

1     Have pity on me, O God, in keeping with your mercy.
      In keeping with your unlimited compassion,
        wipe out my rebellious acts.

²   Wash me thoroughly from my guilt,
     and cleanse me from my sin.
³       I admit that I am rebellious.
       My sin is always in front of me.
⁴   I have sinned against you, especially you.
     I have done what you consider evil.
       So you hand down justice when you speak,
        and you are blameless when you judge.

⁵   Indeed, I was born guilty.
     I was a sinner when my mother conceived me.
⁶   Yet, you desire truth and sincerity.[a]
     Deep down inside me you teach me wisdom.
⁷   Purify me from sin with hyssop,[b] and I will be clean.[c]
     Wash me, and I will be whiter than snow.
⁸      Let me hear ⌊sounds of⌋ joy and gladness.
       Let the bones that you have broken dance.
⁹   Hide your face from my sins,
     and wipe out all that I have done wrong.

¹⁰   Create a clean heart in me, O God,
     and renew a faithful spirit within me.
¹¹   Do not force me away from your presence,
     and do not take your Holy Spirit from me.
¹²   Restore the joy of your salvation to me,
     and provide me with a spirit of willing obedience.

¹³      ⌊Then⌋ I will teach your ways
       to those who are rebellious,
      and sinners will return to you.
¹⁴   Rescue me from the guilt of murder,
     O God, my savior.

---

[a] 51:6 Hebrew meaning uncertain.   [b] 51:7 Branches from the hyssop plant were used in purification rites.
[c] 51:7 "Clean" refers to anything that Moses' Teachings say is presentable to God.

Let my tongue sing joyfully
about your righteousness!
15 O Lord, open my lips,
and my mouth will tell about your praise.
16 You are not happy with any sacrifice.
Otherwise, I would offer one ˌto youˌ.
You are not pleased with burnt offerings.
17 The sacrifice pleasing to God is a broken spirit.
O God, you do not despise a broken
and sorrowful heart.
18 Favor Zion with your goodness.
Rebuild the walls of Jerusalem.
19 Then you will be pleased with sacrifices offered
in the right spirit—
with burnt offerings and whole burnt offerings.
Young bulls will be offered on your altar.

## PROVERBS 10:24-32

### Righteous People Contrasted to Wicked People

24 That which wicked people dread happens to them,
but ˌthe Lordˌ grants the desire
of righteous people.
25 When the storm has passed,
the wicked person has vanished,
but the righteous person has
an everlasting foundation.
26 Like vinegar to the teeth,
like smoke to the eyes,
so is the lazy person to those who send him
ˌon a missionˌ.
27 The fear of the Lord lengthens ˌthe number ofˌ days,
but the years of wicked people are shortened.

28   The hope of righteous people ⌊leads to⌋ joy,
      but the eager waiting of wicked people comes
         to nothing.

29   The way of the LORD is a fortress
      for an innocent person
      but a ruin to those who are troublemakers.

30   A righteous person will never be moved,
      but wicked people will not continue to live
         in the land.

31   The mouth of a righteous person increases wisdom,
      but a devious tongue will be cut off.

32   The lips of a righteous person announce good will,
      but the mouths of wicked people are devious.

# *Day 29* ≈

## PSALM 52

For the choir director; a *maskil*; a psalm by David when Doeg (who was from Edom) told Saul that David had come to Ahimelech's home.

1   Why do you brag about the evil you've done,
      you hero?
      The mercy of God lasts all day long!

2   Your tongue makes up threats.
      It's like a sharp razor, you master of deceit.

3   You prefer evil to good.
      You prefer lying to speaking the truth.     *Selah*

4   You love every destructive accusation,
      you deceitful tongue!

⁵ But God will ruin you forever.
   He will grab you and drag you out of your tent.
   He will pull your roots out of this world
        of the living.                                    *Selah*
⁶    Righteous people will see ⸢this⸣
        and be struck with fear.
     They will laugh at you and say,
⁷        "Look at this person who refused to make
              God his fortress!
         Instead, he trusted his great wealth
              and became strong through his greed."

⁸ But I am like a large olive tree in God's house.
   I trust the mercy of God forever and ever.
⁹    I will give thanks to you forever
        for what you have done.
     In the presence of your godly people,
        I will wait with hope in your good name.


## PSALM 53ᵃ

For the choir director; according to *mahalath*,ᵇ a *maskil* by David.

¹    Godless fools say in their hearts,
        "There is no God."
     They are corrupt.
     They do disgusting things.
        There is no one who does good things.
²    God looks down from heaven
        on Adam's descendants
     to see if there is anyone who acts wisely,
        if there is anyone who seeks help from God.

---

ᵃ 53:1 Psalm 53 is virtually identical in wording to Psalm 14.  ᵇ 53:1 Unknown musical term.

3     Everyone has fallen away.
          Together they have become rotten to the core.
             No one, not even one person,
                does good things.
4   Are all those troublemakers,
          those who devour my people
             as if they were devouring food,
                so ignorant that they do not call on God?
5   There they are—panic-stricken—
          ⌊but⌋ there was no reason to panic,
             because God has scattered the bones
                of those who set up camp against you.[a]
    You put them to shame.
          After all, God has rejected them.

6   If only salvation for Israel would come from Zion!
    When God restores the fortunes of his people,
          Jacob will rejoice.
             Israel will be glad.


## PSALM 54

For the choir director; on stringed instruments; a *maskil*
by David when people from the city of Ziph told Saul
that David was hiding among them.

1   O God, save me by your name,
          and defend me with your might.
2   O God, hear my prayer,
          and open your ears to the words from my mouth.

3   Strangers have attacked me.
    Ruthless people seek my life.
          They do not think about God.[b]                    *Selah*

---

[a] 53:5 Hebrew meaning uncertain.   [b] 54:3 Hebrew meaning of this line uncertain.

4  God is my helper!
   The Lord is the provider for my life.
5      My enemies spy on me.
           Pay them back with evil.
           Destroy them with your truth!

6  I will make a sacrifice to you along
       with a freewill offering.
   I will give thanks to your good name, O LORD.
7      Your name rescues me from every trouble.
           My eyes will gloat over my enemies.


## PROVERBS 11:1-9

### The Value of Righteousness

1  Dishonest scales are disgusting to the LORD,
       but accurate weights are pleasing to him.
2  Arrogance comes,
       then comes shame,
           but wisdom remains with humble people.
3  Integrity guides decent people,
       but hypocrisy leads treacherous people to ruin.

4  Riches are of no help on the day of fury,
       but righteousness saves from death.
5  The righteousness of innocent people
       makes their road smooth,
           but wicked people fall by their own wickedness.
6  Decent people are saved by their righteousness,
       but treacherous people are trapped
           by their own greed.
7      At the death of a wicked person, hope vanishes.
       Moreover, his confidence in strength vanishes.

8    A righteous person is rescued from trouble,
        and a wicked person takes his place.
9    With his talk a godless person can ruin his neighbor,
        but righteous people are rescued by knowledge.

# *Day 30* ≈

## PSALM 55

For the choir director; on stringed instruments; a *maskil*
by David.

1    Open your ears to my prayer, O God.
        Do not hide from my plea for mercy.
2    Pay attention to me, and answer me.
            My thoughts are restless, and I am confused
3                because my enemy shouts at me
                    and a wicked person persecutes me.
                        They bring misery crashing down on me,
                            and they attack me out of anger.
4    My heart is in turmoil.
        The terrors of death have seized me.
5    Fear and trembling have overcome me.
        Horror has overwhelmed me.
6    I said, "If only I had wings like a dove—
        I would fly away and find rest.
7    Indeed, I would run far away.
        I would stay in the desert.                    *Selah*
8    I would hurry to find shelter
        from the raging wind and storm."

9    Completely confuse their language, O Lord,
        because I see violence and conflict in the city.

10 Day and night they go around
         on ˌtop ofˌ the city walls.
     Trouble and misery are everywhere.
11      Destruction is everywhere.
     Oppression and fraud never leave the streets.[a]

12 If an enemy had insulted me,
     then I could bear it.
     If someone who hated me had attacked me,
     then I could hide from him.
13 But it is you, my equal,
     my best friend,
         one I knew so well!
14          We used to talk to each other
         in complete confidence
     and walk into God's house
         with the festival crowds.

15 Let death suddenly take ˌwicked peopleˌ!
     Let them go into the grave while they are still alive,
         because evil lives in their homes
         as well as in their hearts.
16 But I call on God,
     and the LORD saves me.
17 Morning, noon, and night I complain and groan,
     and he listens to my voice.
18 With ˌhisˌ peace, he will rescue my soul
     from the war waged against me,
         because there are many ˌsoldiers
         fightingˌ against me.
19 God will listen.

---

[a] 55:11 Or "its marketplace."

The one who has sat enthroned
   from the beginning
   will deal with them.       *Selah*
      They never change. They never fear God.

20 ⌊My best friend⌋ has betrayed his friends.
   He has broken his solemn promise.
21    His speech is smoother than butter,
      but there is war in his heart.
   His words are more soothing than oil,
      but they are like swords ready to attack.
22 Turn your burdens over to the LORD,
   and he will take care of you.
      He will never let the righteous person stumble.
23 But you, O God, will throw ⌊wicked people⌋
   into the deepest pit.
   Bloodthirsty and deceitful people
      will not live out half their days.
      But I will trust you.

## PROVERBS 11:10-19

10 When righteous people prosper, a city is glad.
   When wicked people die, there are songs of joy.
11    With the blessing of decent people
      a city is raised up,
   but by the words of wicked people,
      it is torn down.

12 A person who despises a neighbor has no sense,
   but a person who has understanding keeps quiet.
13 Whoever gossips gives away secrets,
   but whoever is trustworthy in spirit
      can keep a secret.
14 A nation will fall when there is no direction,

but with many advisers there is victory.
15 Whoever guarantees a stranger's loan will get
into trouble,
but whoever hates the closing of a deal
remains secure.
16 A gracious woman wins respect,
but ruthless men gain riches.
17 A merciful person helps himself,
but a cruel person hurts himself.
18 A wicked person earns dishonest wages,
but whoever spreads righteousness
earns honest pay.
19 As righteousness leads to life,
so whoever pursues evil finds his own death.

# *Day 31* &#x223B;

## PSALM 56

For the choir director; according to *yonath elem rechokim;*[a]
a *miktam* by David when the Philistines captured him
in Gath.

1 Have pity on me, O God,
because people are harassing me.
All day long warriors oppress me.
2 All day long my enemies spy on me.
They harass me.

---

[a] 56:1 Unknown musical term.

There are so many fighting against me.
<sup>3</sup> Even when I am afraid, I still trust you.

<sup>4</sup>     I praise the word of God.
    I trust God.
    I am not afraid.
       What can mere flesh ˌand bloodˌ do to me?

<sup>5</sup> All day long my enemies twist my words.
    Their every thought is an evil plan against me.
<sup>6</sup> They attack, and then they hide.
    They watch my every step as they wait
       to take my life.
<sup>7</sup> With the wrong they do, can they escape?
    O God, angrily make the nations fall.
<sup>8</sup>    (You have kept a record of my wanderings.
       Put my tears in your bottle.
         They are already in your book.)
<sup>9</sup> Then my enemies will retreat when I call ˌto youˌ.
    This I know: God is on my side.

<sup>10</sup>    I praise the word of God.
    I praise the word of the LORD.
<sup>11</sup>    I trust God.
    I am not afraid.
       What can mortals do to me?

<sup>12</sup> I am bound by my vows to you, O God.
    I will keep my vows by offering songs
       of thanksgiving to you.
<sup>13</sup>    You have rescued me from death.
    You have kept my feet from stumbling
       so that I could walk in your presence,
         in the light of life.

## PSALM 57

For the choir director; *al tashcheth;*[a] a *miktam* by David when he fled from Saul into the cave.

1    Have pity on me, O God. Have pity on me,
         because my soul takes refuge in you.
             I will take refuge in the shadow of your wings
                 until destructive storms pass by.
2    I call to God Most High,
         to the God who does everything for me.
3    He sends his help from heaven and saves me.
     He disgraces the one who is harassing me.        *Selah*
     God sends his mercy and his truth!
4    My soul is surrounded by lions.
     I must lie down with man-eating lions.
         Their teeth are spears and arrows.
         Their tongues are sharp swords.
5            May you be honored above the heavens,
                 O God.
             Let your glory extend over the whole earth.

6    ⌊My enemies⌋ spread out a net to catch me.
         (My soul is bowed down.)[b]
     They dug a pit to trap me,
         but then they fell into it.                  *Selah*

7    My heart is confident, O God.
     My heart is confident.
     I want to sing and make music.[c]
8        Wake up, my soul![d]
         Wake up, harp and lyre!
     I want to wake up at dawn.

---

[a] 57:1 Unknown musical term.   [b] 57:6 Hebrew meaning of this line uncertain.   [c] 57:7 Verses 7-11 are virtually identical in wording to Psalm 108:1-5.   [d] 57:8 Or "my glory."

⁹ I want to give thanks to you among the people,
    O Lord.
  I want to make music to praise you
    among the nations
¹⁰   because your mercy is as high as the heavens.
    Your truth reaches the skies.

¹¹     May you be honored above the heavens,
        O God.
    Let your glory extend over the whole earth.

### PROVERBS 11:20-31

²⁰ Devious people are disgusting to the LORD,
    but he is delighted with those
        whose ways are innocent.
²¹ Certainly, an evil person will not go unpunished,
    but the descendants of righteous people
        will escape.
²² ⸢Like⸣ a gold ring in a pig's snout,
    ⸢so⸣ is a beautiful woman who lacks good taste.
²³ The desire of righteous people ends only in good,
    but the hope of wicked people ends only in fury.

²⁴ One person spends freely and yet grows richer,
    while another holds back what he owes
        and yet grows poorer.
²⁵     A generous person will be made rich,
        and whoever satisfies others
            will himself be satisfied.[a]
²⁶ People will curse the one who hoards grain,
    but a blessing will be upon the head of the one
        who sells it.

---

[a] 11:25 Or "and whoever gives someone a drink will also get a drink."

27 Whoever eagerly seeks good searches
for good will,
but whoever looks for evil finds it.
28 Whoever trusts his riches will fall,
but righteous people will flourish like a green leaf.
29 Whoever brings trouble upon his family
inherits ⌊only⌋ wind,
and that stubborn fool becomes a slave
to the wise in heart.
30 The fruit of a righteous person is a tree of life,
and a winner of souls is wise.
31 If the righteous person is rewarded on earth,
how much more the wicked person
and the sinner!

# Day 32 ❧

## PSALM 58

For the choir director; *al tashcheth*; a *miktam* by David.

1 Do you rulers really give fair verdicts?
Do you judge Adam's descendants fairly?
2 No, you invent new crimes on earth,
and your hands spread violence.

3 ⌊Even⌋ inside the womb wicked people
are strangers ⌊to God⌋.
From their birth liars go astray.
4 They have poisonous venom like snakes.
They are like a deaf cobra that shuts its ears
5 so that it cannot hear the voice

of a snake charmer
or of anyone trained to cast spells.

6  O God, knock the teeth out of their mouths.
   Break the young lions' teeth, O LORD.
7  Let them disappear like water that drains away.
   When they aim their bows,
      let their arrows miss the target.[a]
8  Let them become like a snail
      that leaves behind a slimy trail
   or like a stillborn child who never sees the sun.
9  Let ˻God˼ sweep them away
      faster than a cooking pot is heated
         by burning twigs.[b]

10 Righteous people will rejoice
      when they see ˻God˼ take revenge.
   They will wash their feet
      in the blood of wicked people.
11 Then people will say,
      "Righteous people certainly have a reward.
   There is a God who judges on earth."

## PSALM 59

For the choir director; *al tashcheth*; a *miktam* by David
when Saul sent men to watch David's home and kill him.

1  Rescue me from my enemies, O my God.
      Protect me from those who attack me.
2  Rescue me from troublemakers.
      Save me from bloodthirsty people.
3       They lie in ambush for me right here!
      Fierce men attack me, O LORD,

---

[a] 58:7 Hebrew meaning of this sentence uncertain.  [b] 58:9 Hebrew meaning uncertain.

4        but not because of any disobedience,
          or any sin, or any guilt on my part.
       They hurry to take positions against me.
Wake up, and help me; see ⸢for yourself⸣.

5  O LORD God of Armies, God of Israel,
     arise to punish all the nations.
     Have no pity on any traitors.         *Selah*

6        They return in the evening.
       They howl like dogs.
       They prowl the city.

7  See what pours out of their mouths—
     swords from their lips!
       ⸢They think,⸣ "Who will hear us?"

8  O LORD, you laugh at them.
     You make fun of all the nations.

9      O my strength, I watch for you!
       God is my stronghold, my merciful God!

10  God will come to meet me.
He will let me gloat over those who spy on me.
11  Do not kill them.
     Otherwise, my people may forget.
Make them wander aimlessly by your power.
Bring them down, O Lord, our shield,
12     ⸢because of⸣ the sins from their mouths
     and the words on their lips.
Let them be trapped by their own arrogance
     because they speak curses and lies.
13  Destroy them in your rage.
Destroy them until not one of them is left.
     Then they will know that God rules Jacob
      to the ends of the earth.       *Selah*

14      They return in the evening.
        They howl like dogs.
        They prowl the city.

15  They wander around to find something to eat.
        If they are not full enough,
            they will stay all night.
16  But I will sing about your strength.
        In the morning I will joyfully sing
            about your mercy.
        You have been my stronghold
            and a place of safety in times of trouble.

17      O my strength, I will make music to praise you!
        God is my stronghold, my merciful God!

## PROVERBS 12:1-7

1   Whoever loves discipline loves to learn,
        but whoever hates correction is a dumb animal.
2   A good person obtains favor from the LORD,
        but the LORD condemns everyone who schemes.
3   A person cannot stand firm on a foundation
            of wickedness,
        and the roots of righteous people
            cannot be moved.
4   A wife with strength of character is the crown
            of her husband,
        but the wife who disgraces him
            is like bone cancer.

5   The thoughts of righteous people are fair.
    The advice of wicked people is treacherous.
6       The words of wicked people
            are a deadly ambush,

but the words[a] of decent people rescue.
7 Overthrow wicked people, and they are no more,
but the families of righteous people continue
to stand.

# *Day 33* ❧

## PSALM 60

For the choir director; according to *shushan eduth*;[b]
a *miktam* by David; for teaching. When David fought Aram
Naharaim and Aram Zobah, and ˎwhenˎ Joab came back
and killed 12,000 men from Edom in the Dead Sea region.

1 O God, you have rejected us.
    You have broken down our defenses.
    You have been angry.
    Restore us!
2 You made the land quake.
    You split it wide open.
      Heal the cracks in it
        because it is falling apart.
3 You have made your people experience hardships.
    You have given us wine that makes us stagger.
4 Yet, you have raised a flag for those who fear you
    so that they can rally to it
      when attacked by bows ˎand arrowsˎ.          *Selah*
5 Save ˎusˎ with your powerful hand, and answer us
    so that those who are dear to you
      may be rescued.[c]

---

[a] 12:6 Or "mouths."   [b] 60:1 Unknown musical term.   [c] 60:5 Verses 5-12 are virtually identical in
wording to Psalm 108:6-13.

<sup>6</sup> God has promised the following through his holiness:
> "I will triumph!
>> I will divide Shechem.
>> I will measure the valley of Succoth.

<sup>7</sup>
>> Gilead is mine.
>> Manasseh is mine.
>> Ephraim is the helmet on my head.
>> Judah is my scepter.

<sup>8</sup>
>> Moab is my washtub.
>> I will throw my shoe over Edom.
>> I will shout in triumph over Philistia."

<sup>9</sup> Who will bring me into the fortified city?
Who will lead me to Edom?

<sup>10</sup> Isn't it you, O God, who rejected us?
Isn't it you, O God,
who refused to accompany our armies?

<sup>11</sup> Give us help against the enemy
because human assistance is worthless.

<sup>12</sup> With God we will display great strength.
He will trample our enemies.

## PSALM 61

For the choir director; on a stringed instrument; by David.

<sup>1</sup> Listen to my cry for help, O God.
Pay attention to my prayer.

<sup>2</sup> From the ends of the earth, I call to you
when I begin to lose heart.
Lead me to the rock that is high above me.

<sup>3</sup> You have been my refuge,
a tower of strength against the enemy.

<sup>4</sup> I would like to be a guest in your tent forever

and to take refuge under the protection
        of your wings.                                    *Selah*
5    O God, you have heard my vows.
            You have given me the inheritance
                that belongs to those who fear your name.
6   Add days upon days to the life of the king.
    May his years endure throughout every generation.
7   May he sit enthroned
            in the presence of God forever.
    May mercy and truth protect him.
8       Then I will make music
                to praise your name forever,
                as I keep my vows day after day.


## PROVERBS 12:8-20

8   A person will be praised based on his insight,
            but whoever has a twisted mind will be despised.
9   Better to be unimportant and have a slave
            than to act important and have nothing to eat.
10  A righteous person cares ⌞even⌟ about the life
                of his animals,
            but the compassion of wicked people
                is ⌞nothing but⌟ cruelty.
11  Whoever works his land will have plenty to eat,
            but the one who chases unrealistic dreams
                has no sense.
12  A wicked person delights in setting a trap
                for ⌞other⌟ evil people,
            but the roots of righteous people produce ⌞fruit⌟.*a*
13  An evil person is trapped by his own sinful talk,
            but a righteous person escapes from trouble.

---

*a* 12:12 Hebrew meaning of this verse uncertain.

14 One person enjoys good things as a result
   of his speaking ability.
   Another is paid
   according to what his hands have accomplished.

15 A stubborn fool considers his own way the right one,
   but a person who listens to advice is wise.
16 When a stubborn fool is irritated,
   he shows it immediately,
   but a sensible person hides the insult.

17 A truthful witness speaks honestly,
   but a lying witness speaks deceitfully.
18 Careless words stab like a sword,
   but the words of wise people bring healing.
19 The word of truth lasts forever,
   but lies last only a moment.
20 Deceit is in the heart of those who plan evil,
   but joy belongs to those who advise peace.


# *Day 34* ≈

## PSALM 62

For the choir director; according to Jeduthun; a psalm by David.

1 My soul waits calmly for God alone.
   My salvation comes from him.
2 He alone is my rock and my savior—my stronghold.
   I cannot be severely shaken.

3 How long will all of you attack a person?
How long will you try to murder him,
as though he were a leaning wall
or a sagging fence?
4     They plan to force him out of his high position.
They are happy to lie.
They bless with their mouths,
but in their hearts they curse.     *Selah*

5 Wait calmly for God alone, my soul,
because my hope comes from him.
6 He alone is my rock and my savior—my stronghold.
I cannot be shaken.

7 My salvation and my glory depend on God.
God is the rock of my strength, my refuge.
8 Trust him at all times, you people.
Pour out your hearts in his presence.
God is our refuge.     *Selah*

9 Common people are only a whisper in the wind.
Important people are only a delusion.
When all of them are weighed on a scale,
they amount to nothing.
They are less than a whisper in the wind.
10 Do not count on extortion ˌto make you richˌ.
Do not hope to gain anything through robbery.
When riches increase, do not depend on them.

11 God has spoken once.
I have heard it ˌsaidˌ twice:
"Power belongs to God.
12         Mercy belongs to you, O Lord.
You reward a person based on what
he has done."

## PSALM 63

A psalm by David when he was in the wilderness of Judah.

¹  O God, you are my God.
　　At dawn I search for you.
　　　My soul thirsts for you.
　　　My body longs for you
　　　　in a dry, parched land
　　　　　where there is no water.
²  So I look for you in the holy place
　　to see your power and your glory.
³  My lips will praise you
　　because your mercy is better than life ˌitselfˌ.
⁴  So I will thank you as long as I live.
　　I will lift up my hands ˌto prayˌ in your name.
⁵  You satisfy my soul with the richest foods.
　　My mouth will sing ˌyourˌ praise with joyful lips.
⁶  As I lie on my bed, I remember you.
　　Through the long hours of the night,
　　　I think about you.
⁷  You have been my help.
　　In the shadow of your wings, I sing joyfully.
⁸  My soul clings to you.
　　Your right hand supports me.

⁹  But those who try to destroy my life
　　will go into the depths of the earth.
¹⁰　　They will be cut down by swords.
　　　Their dead bodies will be left
　　　　as food for jackals.
¹¹  But the king will find joy in God.
　　Everyone who takes an oath by God will brag,
　　　but the mouths of liars will be shut.

## PROVERBS 12:21-28

21 No ⸢lasting⸣ harm comes to a righteous person,
    but wicked people have lots of trouble.

22 Lips that lie are disgusting to the LORD,
    but honest people are his delight.

23 A sensible person ⸢discreetly⸣ hides knowledge,
    but foolish minds preach stupidity.

24 Hard-working hands gain control,
    but lazy hands do slave labor.

25 A person's anxiety will weigh him down,
    but an encouraging word makes him joyful.

26 A righteous person looks out for his neighbor,
    but the path of wicked people leads others astray.

27 A lazy hunter does not catch[a] his prey,
    but a hard-working person becomes wealthy.[b]

28 Everlasting life is on the way of righteousness.
    Eternal death is not along its path.

# *Day 35* ❧

## PSALM 64

For the choir director; a psalm by David.

1 Hear my voice, O God, when I complain.
    Protect my life from a terrifying enemy.

2 Hide me from the secret plots of criminals,
    from the mob of troublemakers.

3     They sharpen their tongues like swords.
        They aim bitter words like arrows

---

[a] 12:27 Hebrew meaning uncertain.   [b] 12:27 Hebrew meaning of this line uncertain.

4      to shoot at innocent people
          from their hiding places.
      They shoot at them suddenly, without any fear.

5      They encourage one another in their evil plans.
      They talk about setting traps and say,
          "Who can see them?"

6      They search for the perfect crime and say,
          "We have perfected a foolproof scheme!"
      Human nature and the human heart
          are a mystery!

7  But God will shoot them with an arrow.
      Suddenly, they will be struck dead.

8  They will trip over their own tongues.
      Everyone who sees them will shake his head.

9  Everyone will be afraid and conclude,
      "This is an act of God!"
      They will learn from what he has done.

10  Righteous people will find joy in the LORD
      and take refuge in him.
      Everyone whose motives are decent
      will be able to brag.

## PSALM 65

For the choir director; a psalm by David; a song.

1  You are praised with silence in Zion, O God,
      and vows ˌmadeˌ to you must be kept.

2  You are the one who hears prayers.
      Everyone will come to you.

3  Various sins overwhelm me.
      You are the one who forgives our rebellious acts.

4  Blessed is the person you choose

and invite to live with you in your courtyards.
   We will be filled with good food
      from your house,
      from your holy temple.

⁵ You answer us with awe-inspiring acts
      ⌞done⌟ in righteousness,
   O God, our savior,
      the hope of all the ends of the earth
         and of the most distant sea,
⁶      the one who set the mountains in place
         with his strength,
      the one who is clothed with power,
⁷      the one who calms the roar of the seas,
         their crashing waves,
            and the uproar of the nations.
⁸ Those who live at the ends of the earth are in awe
      of your miraculous signs.
   The lands of the morning sunrise and evening sunset
      sing joyfully.

⁹ You take care of the earth, and you water it.
   You make it much richer than it was.
      (The river of God is filled with water.)
   You provide grain for them.
      Indeed, you even prepare the ground.
¹⁰ You drench plowed fields ⌞with rain⌟
      and level their clumps of soil.
   You soften them with showers
      and bless what grows in them.
¹¹ You crown the year with your goodness,
      and richness overflows wherever you are.
¹²      The pastures in the desert overflow
            ⌞with richness⌟.

The hills are surrounded with joy.
13  The pastures are covered with flocks.
The valleys are carpeted with grain.
All of them shout triumphantly.
Indeed, they sing.

## PROVERBS 13:1-6

### A Wise Son Lives Righteously

1  A wise son listens to his father's discipline,
    but a mocker does not listen to reprimands.
2  A person eats well as a result of his speaking ability,
    but the appetite of treacherous people
        ˌcravesˌ violence.
3  Whoever controls his mouth protects his own life.
    Whoever has a big mouth comes to ruin.
4  A lazy person craves food and there is none,
    but the appetite of hard-working people
        is satisfied.
5  A righteous person hates lying,
    but a wicked person behaves with shame
        and disgrace.
6  Righteousness protects the honest way of life,
    but wickedness ruins a sacrifice for sin.

# Day 36 ≈

## PSALM 66

For the choir director; a song; a psalm.

1  Shout happily to God, all the earth!
2  Make music to praise the glory of his name.

Make his praise glorious.

3 Say to God,
  "How awe-inspiring are your deeds!
  Your power is so great
    that your enemies will cringe in front of you.

4 The whole earth will worship you.
    It will make music to praise you.
    It will make music to praise your name."    *Selah*

5 Come and see what God has done—
    his awe-inspiring deeds for Adam's descendants.

6 He turned the sea into dry land.
    They crossed the river on foot.
      We rejoiced because of what he did there.

7 He rules forever with his might.
    His eyes watch the nations.
      Rebels will not be able to oppose him.    *Selah*

8 Thank our God, you nations.
  Make the sound of his praise heard.

9   He has kept us alive
    and has not allowed us to fall.

10 You have tested us, O God.
  You have refined us in the same way silver is refined.

11 You have trapped us in a net.
  You have laid burdens on our backs.

12 You let people ride over our heads.
    We went through fire and water,
      but then you brought us out and refreshed us.

13 I will come into your temple with burnt offerings.
  I will keep my vows to you,

14    the vows made by my lips and spoken
        by my ˻own˼ mouth
      when I was in trouble.

15    I will offer you a sacrifice of fattened livestock
       for burnt offerings
     with the smoke from rams.
   I will offer cattle and goats.              *Selah*

16    Come and listen, all who fear God,
       and I will tell you what he has done for me.
17        With my mouth I cried out to him.
         High praise was on my tongue.
18    If I had thought about doing anything sinful,
       the Lord would not have listened to me.
19    But God has heard me.
       He has paid attention to my prayer.

20    Thanks be to God,
       who has not rejected my prayer
         or taken away his mercy from me.

## PSALM 67

For the choir director; on stringed instruments; a psalm;
a song.

1    May God have pity on us and bless us!
   May he smile on us.                 *Selah*
2      Then your ways will be known on earth,
       your salvation throughout all nations.

3    Let everyone give thanks to you, O God.
   Let everyone give thanks to you.
4    Let the nations be glad and sing joyfully
       because you judge everyone with justice
         and guide the nations on the earth.     *Selah*
5    Let the people give thanks to you, O God.
   Let all the people give thanks to you.
6      The earth has yielded its harvest.

May God, our God, bless us.

⁷ May God bless us,
     and may all the ends of the earth worship him.

### PROVERBS 13:7-18

⁷ One person pretends to be rich but has nothing.
     Another pretends to be poor
         but has great wealth.

⁸ A person's riches are the ransom for his life,
     but the poor person does not pay attention
         to threats.

⁹ The light of righteous people beams brightly,
     but the lamp of wicked people will be snuffed out.

¹⁰ Arrogance produces only quarreling,
     but those who take advice gain wisdom.

¹¹ Wealth ˻gained˼ through injustice dwindles away,
     but whoever gathers little by little has plenty.

¹² Delayed hope makes one sick at heart,
     but a fulfilled longing is a tree of life.

¹³ Whoever despises ˻God's˼ words will pay the penalty,
     but the one who fears ˻God's˼ commands
         will be rewarded.

¹⁴ The teachings of a wise person are a fountain of life
     to turn ˻one˼ away from the grasp of death.

¹⁵ Good sense brings favor,
     but the way of treacherous people is always
         the same.ᵃ

¹⁶ Any sensible person acts with knowledge,
     but a fool displays stupidity.

¹⁷ An undependable messenger gets into trouble,
     but a dependable envoy brings healing.

---

ᵃ 13:15 Masoretic Text; Greek "is their disaster."

<sup>18</sup> Poverty and shame come to a person
　　who ignores discipline,
　　but whoever pays attention
　　　　to constructive criticism will be honored.

# *Day 37* ≈

## PSALM 68

For the choir director; a psalm by David; a song.

<sup>1</sup>　God will arise.
　　His enemies will be scattered.
　　Those who hate him will flee from him.
<sup>2</sup>　　Blow them away like smoke.
　　　Let wicked people melt in God's presence
　　　　like wax next to a fire.

<sup>3</sup>　But let righteous people rejoice.
　　　Let them celebrate in God's presence.
　　　Let them overflow with joy.
<sup>4</sup>　Sing to God; make music to praise his name.
　　Make a highway for him to ride through the deserts.<sup>a</sup>
　　　The LORD is his name.
　　Celebrate in his presence.

<sup>5</sup>　The God who is in his holy dwelling place
　　　is the father of the fatherless
　　　　and the defender of widows.
<sup>6</sup>　God places lonely people in families.
　　　He leads prisoners out of prison
　　　　into productive lives,

---

<sup>a</sup> 68:4 Or "Lift a song to him who rides upon the clouds."

but rebellious people must live
in an unproductive land.

7  O God, when you went in front of your people,
when you marched through the desert,      *Selah*
8       the earth quaked and the sky poured
in the presence of the God of Sinai,
in the presence of the God of Israel.

9  You watered the land with plenty of rain, O God.
You refreshed it when your land was exhausted.
10      Your flock settled there.
Out of your goodness, O God,
you provided for oppressed people.

11  The Lord gives instructions.
The women who announce the good news
are a large army.
12      ₁They say,₁ "The kings of the armies flee;
they run away.
The women who remained at home
will divide the goods.
13          Though you stayed
among the sheep pens,
₁you will be like₁ the wings of a dove
covered with silver,
its feathers with yellow gold.
14          Meanwhile, the Almighty was still scattering
kings there
like snow falling on Mount Zalmon."

15  The mountain of Bashan is the mountain of God.
The mountain of Bashan is the mountain
with many peaks.
16      Why do you look with envy, you mountains

with many peaks,
  at the mountain where God has chosen to live?
  Certainly, the LORD will live there forever.

17  The chariots of God are twenty thousand in number,
      thousands upon thousands.
    The Lord is among them.
      The God of Sinai is in his holy place.

18  You went to the highest place.
    You took prisoners captive.
    You received gifts from people,
      even from rebellious people,
        so that the LORD God may live there.

19  Thanks be to the Lord,
      who daily carries our burdens for us.
        God is our salvation.                    *Selah*

20  Our God is the God of victories.
    The Almighty LORD is our escape from death.

21  Certainly, God will crush the heads of his enemies
      and destroy even the hair on the heads
        of those who continue to be guilty.

22  The Lord said, "I will bring them back from Bashan.
      I will bring them back from the depths of the sea

23      so that you, my people, may bathe*a*
          your feet in blood
        and the tongues of your dogs
          may lick the blood of your enemies."

24  Your festival processions, O God,
      can be seen by everyone.
    They are the processions for my God, my king,
      into the holy place.

---

*a* 68:23 Greek, Targum, Syriac; Masoretic Text "shatter."

25      The singers are in front.
     The musicians are behind them.
     The young women beating tambourines
         are between them.

26         Thank God, the Lord, the source of Israel,
           with the choirs.

27         Benjamin, the youngest, is leading them,
       ˌnextˌ the leaders of Judah
          with their noisy crowds,
       ˌthenˌ the leaders of Zebulun,
       ˌthenˌ the leaders of Naphtali.

28 Your God has decided you will be strong.
     Display your strength, O God,
       as you have for us before.

29 Kings will bring you gifts
     because of your temple high above Jerusalem.

30 Threaten the beast who is among the cattails,
     the herd of bulls with the calves of the nations,
       until it humbles itself with pieces of silver.
Scatter the people who find joy in war.[a]

31 Ambassadors will come from Egypt.
Sudan will stretch out its hands to God ˌin prayerˌ.

32 You kingdoms of the world, sing to God.
     Make music to praise the Lord.       *Selah*

33        God rides through the ancient heaven,
         the highest heaven.
     Listen! He makes his voice heard,
       his powerful voice.

---

[a] 68:30 Hebrew meaning of this verse uncertain.

³⁴     Acknowledge the power of God.
          His majesty is over Israel,
               and his power is in the skies.

³⁵  God, the God of Israel, is awe-inspiring
          in his holy place.
       He gives strength and power to his people.
          Thanks be to God!

### PROVERBS 13:19-25

¹⁹  A fulfilled desire is sweet to the soul,
       but turning from evil is disgusting to fools.
²⁰  Whoever walks with wise people will be wise,
       but whoever associates with fools will suffer.
²¹  Disaster hunts down sinners,
       but righteous people are rewarded with good.
²²  Good people leave an inheritance
          to their grandchildren,
       but the wealth of sinners is stored away
          for a righteous person.

²³  When poor people are able to plow,
          there is much food,
       but a person is swept away
          where there is no justice.
²⁴  Whoever refuses to spank his son hates him,
       but whoever loves his son disciplines him
          from early on.
²⁵  A righteous person eats to satisfy his appetite,
       but the bellies of wicked people are always empty.

# *Day 38* ∞

## PSALM 69

For the choir director; according to *shoshannim*; by David.

1　Save me, O God!
　　　The water is already up to my neck!
2　I am sinking in deep mud.
　　　There is nothing to stand on.
　　I am in deep water.
　　　A flood is sweeping me away.
3　I am exhausted from crying for help.
　　　My throat is hoarse.
　　　My eyes are strained ˌfromˌ looking for my God.
4　　　Those who hate me for no reason
　　　　　outnumber the hairs on my head.
　　　Those who want to destroy me are mighty.
　　　　　They have no reason to be my enemies.
　　I am forced to pay back what I did not steal.

5　O God, you know my stupidity,
　　　and the things of which I am guilty
　　　　are not hidden from you.
6　Do not let those who wait with hope for you
　　　be put to shame because of me,
　　　　　O Almighty LORD of Armies.
　　Do not let those who come to you for help
　　　be humiliated because of me, O God of Israel.

7　Indeed, for your sake I have endured insults.
　　　Humiliation has covered my face.

⁸  I have become a stranger to my ˏownˏ brothers,
    a foreigner to my mother's sons.

⁹  Indeed, devotion for your house has consumed me,
    and the insults of those who insult you
        have fallen on me.

¹⁰  I cried and fasted, but I was insulted for it.

¹¹  I dressed myself in sackcloth,
    but I became the object of ridicule.

¹²    Those who sit at the gate gossip about me,
    and drunkards make up songs about me.

¹³    May my prayer come to you at an acceptable time,
    O Lᴏʀᴅ.
    O God, out of the greatness of your mercy,
      answer me with the truth of your salvation.

¹⁴  Rescue me from the mud.
    Do not let me sinkˏintoˏ itˏ.
  I want to be rescued from those who hate me
    and from the deep water.

¹⁵  Do not let floodwaters sweep me away.
    Do not let the ocean swallow me up,
      or the pit close its mouth over me.

¹⁶  Answer me, O Lᴏʀᴅ, because your mercy is good.
  Out of your unlimited compassion, turn to me.

¹⁷  I am in trouble, so do not hide your face from me.
    Answer me quickly!

¹⁸  Come close, and defend my soul.
    Set me free because of my enemies.

¹⁹  You know that I have been insulted,
    put to shame, and humiliated.
  All my opponents are in front of you.

²⁰    Insults have broken my heart, and I am sick.
    I looked for sympathy, but there was none.

      I looked for people to comfort me,
         but I found no one.
**21**        They poisoned my food,
         and when I was thirsty,
           they gave me vinegar to drink.

**22**  Let the table set for them become a trap
      and a snare for their friends.
**23**  Let their vision become clouded
        so that they cannot see.
Let their thighs continually shake.

**24**  Pour your rage on them.
      Let your burning anger catch up with them.
**25**      Let their camp be deserted
        and their tents empty.

**26**  They persecute the one you have struck,
      and they talk about the pain
        of those you have wounded.
**27**  Charge them with one crime after another.
      Do not let them be found innocent.
**28**  Let their ˌnamesˌ be erased from the Book of Life.
      Do not let them be listed with righteous people.

**29**  I am suffering and in pain.
      Let your saving power protect me, O God.
**30**  I want to praise the name of God with a song.
I want to praise its greatness
      with a song of thanksgiving.
**31**      This will please the Lord
        more than ˌsacrificingˌ an ox
      or a bull with horns and hoofs.
**32**  Oppressed people will see ˌthisˌ and rejoice.

May the hearts of those who look to God for help
    be refreshed.
33 The LORD listens to needy people.
He does not despise his own who are in prison.
34 Let heaven and earth, the seas,
    and everything that moves in them, praise him.
35 When God saves Zion,
    he will rebuild the cities of Judah.
    His servants will live there
      and take possession of it.
36     The descendants of his servants will inherit it.
      Those who love him will live there.

## PROVERBS 14:1-13

### Wise People Live Righteously

1 The wisest of women builds up her home,
    but a stupid one tears it down
      with her own hands.
2 Whoever lives right fears the LORD,
    but a person who is devious in his ways
      despises him.
3 Because of a stubborn fool's words
    a whip is lifted against him,
    but wise people are protected by their speech.

4 Where there are no cattle,
    the feeding trough is empty,
    but the strength of an ox
      produces plentiful harvests.
5 A trustworthy witness does not lie,
    but a dishonest witness breathes lies.
6 A mocker searches for wisdom without finding it,

but knowledge comes easily to a person
who has understanding.

7 Stay away from a fool,
because you will not receive knowledge
from his lips.
8 The wisdom of a sensible person guides his way
of life,
but the stupidity of fools misleads them.
9 Stubborn fools make fun of guilt,
but there is forgiveness among decent people.

10 The heart knows its own bitterness,
and no stranger can share its joy.
11 The houses of wicked people will be destroyed,
but the tents of decent people will continue
to expand.
12 There is a way that seems right to a person,
but eventually it ends in death.
13 Even while laughing a heart can ache,
and joy can end in grief.

# *Day 39* ❧

## PSALM 70[a]

For the choir director; by David; to be kept in mind.

1 Come quickly to rescue me, O God!
Come quickly to help me, O LORD!
2 Let those who seek my life
be confused and put to shame.
Let those who want my downfall

[a] 70:1 Psalm 70 is virtually identical in wording to Psalm 40:13-17.

be turned back and disgraced.
³ Let those who say, "Aha! Aha!"
    be turned back because of their own shame.
⁴ Let all who seek you rejoice and be glad
        because of you.
    Let those who love your salvation continually say,
    "God is great!"

⁵ But I am oppressed and needy.
O God, come to me quickly.
    You are my help and my savior.
        O LORD, do not delay!

## PSALM 71

¹ I have taken refuge in you, O LORD.
    Never let me be put to shame.
² Rescue me and free me
        because of your righteousness.
    Turn your ear toward me, and save me.
³     Be a rock on which I may live,
            a place where I may always go.
                You gave the order to save me!
        Indeed, you are my rock and my fortress.
⁴ My God, free me from the hands of a wicked person,
        from the grasp of one who is cruel and unjust.
⁵ You are my hope, O Almighty LORD.
You have been my confidence
        ever since I was young.
⁶ I depended on you before I was born.
    You took me from my mother's womb.
        My songs of praise constantly speak about you.
⁷ I have become an example to many people,
        but you are my strong refuge.

8 My mouth is filled with your praise,
   with your glory all day long.

9 Do not reject me when I am old
   or abandon me when I lose my strength.

10 My enemies talk about me.
   They watch me as they plot to take my life.

11 They say, "God has abandoned him.
   Pursue him and grab him because there is no one
     to rescue him."

12 O God, do not be so distant from me.
   O my God, come quickly to help me.

13 Let those who accuse me come to a shameful end.
   Let those who want my downfall be covered
     with disgrace and humiliation.

14 But I will always have hope.
   I will praise you more and more.

15 My mouth will tell about your righteousness,
   about your salvation all day long.
     Even then, it is more than I can understand.

16 I will come with the mighty deeds
     of the Almighty Lord.
   I will praise your righteousness, yours alone.

17 O God, you have taught me ever since I was young,
   and I still talk about the miracles you have done.

18 Even when I am old and gray, do not abandon me,
     O God.
   Let me live to tell the people of this age
     what your strength has accomplished,
       to tell about your power to all who will come.

19 Your righteousness reaches to the heavens, O God.
   You have done great things.

O God, who is like you?
<sup>20</sup> You have made me endure many terrible troubles.
You restore me to life again.
You bring me back from the depths of the earth.
<sup>21</sup> You comfort me and make me greater than ever.

<sup>22</sup> Because of your faithfulness, O my God,
even I will give thanks to you as I play on a lyre.
I will make music with a harp to praise you,
O Holy One of Israel.
<sup>23</sup> My lips will sing with joy when I make music
to praise you.
My soul, which you have rescued,
also will sing joyfully.
<sup>24</sup> My tongue will tell about your righteousness
all day long,
because those who wanted my downfall
have been disgraced and put to shame.

## PROVERBS 14:14-21

<sup>14</sup> A heart that turns ˌfrom Godˌ becomes bored
with its own ways,
but a good person is satisfied with God's ways.
<sup>15</sup> A gullible person believes anything,
but a sensible person watches his step.
<sup>16</sup> A wise person is cautious and turns away from evil,
but a fool is careless<sup>a</sup> and overconfident.
<sup>17</sup> A short-tempered person acts stupidly,
and a person who plots evil is hated.
<sup>18</sup> Gullible people are gifted with stupidity,
but sensible people are crowned with knowledge.

---

<sup>a</sup> 14:16 Hebrew meaning uncertain.

19 Evil people will bow to good people.
    Wicked people will bow at the gates
        of a righteous person.

20 A poor person is hated even by his neighbor,
        but a rich person is loved by many.
21 Whoever despises his neighbor sins,
        but blessed is the one who is kind
            to humble people.

# *Day 40* ≈

## PSALM 72

By Solomon.

1 O God, give the king your justice
        and the king's son[a] your righteousness
2        so that he may judge your people
            with righteousness
            and your oppressed ⌊people⌋ with justice.

3 May the mountains bring peace to the people
        and the hills bring righteousness.
4 May he grant justice to the people
        who are oppressed.
    May he save the children of needy people
        and crush their oppressor.
5 May they fear you
        as long as the sun and moon ⌊shine⌋—
        throughout every generation.
6 May he be like rain that falls on ⌊freshly⌋ cut grass,
        like showers that water the land.

---

[a] 72:1 According to ancient Jewish and Christian tradition, "king" and "king's son" refer to the Messiah.

7    May righteous people blossom in his day.
     May there be unlimited peace
        until the moon no longer ˌshinesˌ.

8    May he rule from sea to sea,
        from the Euphrates River to the ends of the earth.

9    May the people of the desert kneel in front of him.
     May his enemies lick the dust.

10   May the kings from Tarshish and the islands
        bring presents.
     May the kings from Sheba and Seba bring gifts.

11   May all kings worship him.
     May all nations serve him.

12      He will rescue the needy person who cries for help
        and the oppressed person
          who has no one's help.

13      He will have pity on the poor and needy
        and will save the lives of the needy.

14      He will rescue them from oppression and violence.
        Their blood will be precious in his sight.

15   May he live long.
     May the gold from Sheba be given to him.
     May ˌthe peopleˌ pray for him continually.
     May ˌtheyˌ praise him all day long.

16   May there be plenty of grain in the land.
     May it wave ˌin the breezeˌ on the mountain tops,
        its fruit like ˌthe treetops ofˌ Lebanon.
     May those from the city flourish like the grass
        on the ground.

17   May his name endure forever.
     May his name continue as long as the sun ˌshinesˌ.
     May all nations be blessed through him
        and call him blessed.

18 Thank the LORD God, the God of Israel,
  who alone does miracles.
19 Thanks be to his glorious name forever.
  May the whole earth be filled with his glory.

Amen and amen!

20 The prayers by David, son of Jesse, end here.

## PROVERBS 14:22-35

22 Don't those who stray plan what is evil,
   while those who are merciful and faithful
     plan what is good?
23   In hard work there is always something gained,
     but idle talk leads only to poverty.
24 The crown of wise people is their wealth.
  The stupidity of fools is just that—stupidity!
25   An honest witness saves lives,
     but one who tells lies is dangerous.
26 In the fear of the LORD there is strong confidence,
  and his children will have a place of refuge.
27 The fear of the LORD is a fountain of life
  to turn ⌞one⌟ away from the grasp of death.
28 A large population is an honor for a king,
  but without people a ruler is ruined.

29 A person of great understanding is patient,
  but a short temper is the height of stupidity.
30 A tranquil heart makes for a healthy body,
  but jealousy is ⌞like⌟ bone cancer.
31 Whoever oppresses the poor insults his maker,
  but whoever is kind to the needy honors him.
32 A wicked person is thrown down
   by his own wrongdoing,

but even in his death a righteous person
has a refuge.
33 Wisdom finds rest in the heart
of an understanding person.
Even fools recognize this.[a]

## Wise Ways to Live

34 Righteousness lifts up a nation,
but sin is a disgrace in any society.
35 A king is delighted with a servant who acts wisely,
but he is furious with one who acts shamefully.

# *Day 41* ∻

## PSALM 73

A psalm by Asaph.

1 God is truly good to Israel,
to those whose lives are pure.

2 But my feet had almost stumbled.
They had almost slipped
3 because I was envious of arrogant people
when I saw the prosperity
that wicked people enjoy.

4 They suffer no pain.
Their bodies are healthy.
5 They have no drudgery in their lives
like ordinary people.
They are not plagued ⸢with problems⸣ like others.

---

[a] 14:33 Hebrew meaning of this line uncertain.

6  That is why they wear arrogance like a necklace
      and acts of violence like clothing.
7  Their eyes peer out from their fat faces,[a]
      and their imaginations run wild.
8  They ridicule.
    They speak maliciously.
    They speak arrogantly about oppression.
9  They verbally attack heaven,
      and they order people around on earth.
10 That is why God's people turn to wickedness[b]
      and swallow their words.
11 Then wicked people ask, "What does God know?"
      "Does the Most High know anything?"
12 Look how wicked they are!
      They never have a worry.
        They grow more and more wealthy.

13 I've received no reward for keeping my life pure
      and washing my hands of any blame.
14 I'm plagued ˻with problems˼ all day long,
      and every morning my punishment ˻begins again˼.
15 If I had said, "I will continue to talk like that,"
      I would have betrayed God's people.

16 But when I tried to understand this,
      it was too difficult for me.
17 Only when I came into God's holy place
      did I ˻finally˼ understand what would happen
        to them.

18 You put them in slippery places
      and make them fall into ruin.
19 They are suddenly destroyed.

---
[a] 73:7 Hebrew meaning uncertain.  [b] 73:10 Hebrew meaning uncertain.

They are completely swept away by terror!

20 As ˌsomeoneˌ gets rid of a dream when he wakes up,
    so you, O Lord, get rid of the thought of them
      when you wake up.

21 When my heart was filled with bitterness
    and my mind was seized ˌwith envyˌ,
22     I was stupid, and I did not understand.
      I was like a dumb animal in your presence.
23 Yet, I am always with you.
    You hold on to my right hand.
24     With your advice you guide me,
      and in the end you will take me to glory.
25 As long as I have you,
    I don't need anyone else in heaven or on earth.
26 My body and mind may waste away,
    but God remains the foundation of my life
    and my inheritance forever.
27 Without a doubt, those who are far from you will die.
    You destroy all who are unfaithful to you.

28 Being united with God is my highest good.
    I have made the Almighty LORD my refuge
      so that I may report everything
       that he has done.


## PROVERBS 15:1-9

1 A gentle answer turns away rage,
    but a harsh word stirs up anger.
2 The tongues of wise people give good expression
      to knowledge,
    but the mouths of fools pour out a flood
      of stupidity.

³ The eyes of the LORD are everywhere.
They watch evil people and good people.
⁴ A soothing tongue is a tree of life,
but a deceitful tongue breaks the spirit.
⁵ A stubborn fool despises his father's discipline,
but whoever appreciates a warning
shows good sense.
⁶ Great treasure is in the house of a righteous person,
but trouble comes along with the income
of a wicked person.
⁷ The lips of wise people spread knowledge,
but a foolish attitude does not.

⁸ A sacrifice brought by wicked people is disgusting
to the LORD,
but the prayers of decent people please him.
⁹ The way of wicked people is disgusting to the LORD,
but he loves those who pursue righteousness.

# *Day 42* &#x2766;

## PSALM 74

A *maskil*[a] by Asaph.

¹ Why, O God, have you rejected us forever?
Why does your anger
smolder against the sheep in your care?

² Remember your congregation.
Long ago you made it your own.

---

[a] 74:1 Unknown musical term.

You bought this tribe to be your possession.
    This tribe is Mount Zion,
        where you have made your home.

³ Turn your steps toward*ᵃ* these pathetic ruins.
    The enemy has destroyed everything
        in the holy temple.

⁴ Your opponents have roared
    inside your meeting place.
        They have set up their own emblems as symbols.
⁵     Starting from its entrance, they hacked away
        like a woodcutter in a forest.*ᵇ*
⁶ They smashed all its carved paneling
    with axes and hatchets.
⁷ They burned your holy place to the ground.
    They dishonored the place where you live
        among us.
⁸     They said to themselves, "We will crush them."
    They burned every meeting place of God
        in the land.

⁹ We no longer see miraculous signs.
    There are no prophets anymore.
        No one knows how long this will last.
¹⁰ How long, O God, will the enemy insult us?
Will the enemy despise you forever?
¹¹ Why do you hold back your hand,
    especially your right hand?
        Take your hands out of your pockets.
        Destroy your enemies!*ᶜ*

---

*ᵃ* 74:3 Hebrew meaning uncertain.   *ᵇ* 74:5 Hebrew meaning of this verse uncertain.   *ᶜ* 74:11 Hebrew meaning of this verse uncertain.

¹² And yet, from long ago God has been my king,
the one who has been victorious
throughout the earth.
¹³ You stirred up the sea with your own strength.
You smashed the heads of sea monsters
in the water.
¹⁴ You crushed the heads of Leviathan*ᵃ*
and gave them to the creatures
of the desert for food.
¹⁵ You opened the springs and brooks.
You dried up the ever-flowing rivers.
¹⁶ The day and the night are yours.
You set the moon and the sun in their places.
¹⁷ You determined all the boundaries of the earth.
You created summer and winter.

¹⁸ Remember how the enemy insulted you, O LORD.
Remember how an entire nation of godless fools
despised your name.
¹⁹ Do not hand over the soul of your dove
to wild animals.
Do not forget the life of your oppressed people
forever.
²⁰ Consider your promise*ᵇ*
because every dark corner of the land is filled
with violence.
²¹ Do not let oppressed people come back in disgrace.
Let weak and needy people praise your name.
²² Arise, O God!
Fight for your own cause!
Remember how godless fools insult you all day long.

---

*ᵃ* 74:14 Hebrew meaning uncertain.    *ᵇ* 74:20 Or "covenant."

<sup>23</sup> Do not forget the shouting of your opponents.
Do not forget the uproar made by those
      who attack you.

### PROVERBS 15:10-19

<sup>10</sup> Discipline is a terrible ˻burden˼ to anyone
      who leaves the ˻right˼ path.
      Anyone who hates a warning will die.
<sup>11</sup> If Sheol and Abaddon lie open in front of the Lord
      how much more the human heart!
<sup>12</sup> A mocker does not appreciate a warning.
      He will not go to wise people.

<sup>13</sup> A joyful heart makes a cheerful face,
      but with a heartache comes depression.
<sup>14</sup> The mind of a person who has understanding
         searches for knowledge,
      but the mouths of fools feed on stupidity.
<sup>15</sup> Every day is a terrible day for a miserable person,
      but a cheerful heart has a continual feast.

<sup>16</sup> Better to have a little with the fear of the Lord
      than great treasure and turmoil.
<sup>17</sup> Better to have a dish of vegetables
         where there is love
      than juicy steaks where there is hate.

<sup>18</sup> A hothead stirs up a fight,
      but one who holds his temper calms disputes.
<sup>19</sup> The path of lazy people is like a thorny hedge,
      but the road of decent people
         is an ˻open˼ highway.

# *Day 43* ✤

## PSALM 75

For the choir director; *al tashcheth*; a psalm by Asaph;
a song.

¹ We give thanks to you, O God; we give thanks.
  You are present, and your miracles confirm that.

² When I choose the right time,
    I will judge fairly.
³ When the earth and everyone who lives on it
      begin to melt,
    I will make its foundations as solid as rock.    *Selah*
⁴ I said to those who brag, "Don't brag,"
    and to wicked people,
      "Don't raise your weapons.
⁵      Don't raise your weapons so proudly
        or speak so defiantly."

⁶ The ˌauthorityˌ to reward someone
      does not ˌcomeˌ
    from the east,
      from the west,
        or ˌevenˌ from the wilderness.
⁷ God alone is the judge.
    He punishes one person and rewards another.
⁸ A cup is in the LORD's hand.
    (Its foaming wine is thoroughly mixed with spices.)
  He will empty it,
    ˌandˌ all the wicked people on earth
      will have to drink every last drop.

9    But I will speak about your miracles forever.
        I will make music to praise the God of Jacob.
10   I will destroy all the weapons of wicked people,
            but the weapons of righteous people
                will be raised proudly.

## PSALM 76

For the choir director; on stringed instruments; a psalm
by Asaph; a song.

1    God is known in Judah.
        His name is great in Israel.
2    His tent is in Salem.
        His home is in Zion.
3        There he destroyed flaming arrows,
            shields, swords, and weapons of war.          *Selah*

4    You are the radiant one.
        You are more majestic than the ancient mountains.[a]
5        Brave people were robbed.
            They died.
                None of the warriors were able to lift a hand.
6                At your stern warning, O God of Jacob,
                chariot riders and horses
                    were put to sleep.

7    You alone must be feared!
        Who can stand in your presence
            when you become angry?
8        From heaven you announced a verdict.
            The earth was fearful and silent
9                when you rose to judge, O God,

---

[a] 76:4 Greek, Syriac; Masoretic Text "mountains of prey."

when you rose to save
　　　every oppressed person on earth. *Selah*

10　Even angry mortals will praise you.
　　You will wear the remainder of ˌtheirˌ anger.ᵃ
11　　Make vows to the Lord your God, and keep them.
　　　Let everyone around him bring gifts to the one
　　　　who must be feared.
12　　　He cuts short the lives of influential people.
　　　He terrifies the kings of the earth.


## PROVERBS 15:20-33

### A Wise Son Brings Blessings to Others

20　A wise son makes his father happy,
　　　but a foolish child despises its mother.

21　Stupidity is fun to the one without much sense,
　　　but a person who has understanding
　　　　forges straight ahead.
22　Without advice plans go wrong,
　　　but with many advisers they succeed.
23　A person is delighted to hear an answer
　　　from his own mouth,
　　　and a timely word—oh, how good!

24　The path of life for a wise person leads upward
　　　in order to turn him away from hell below.
25　The Lord tears down the house
　　　of an arrogant person,
　　　but he protects the property of widows.
26　The thoughts of evil people are disgusting to the Lord,
　　　but pleasant words are pure to him.

---

ᵃ 76:10 Hebrew meaning of this line uncertain.

<sup>27</sup> Whoever is greedy for unjust gain brings trouble
    to his family,
      but whoever hates bribes will live.

<sup>28</sup> The heart of a righteous person carefully considers
    how to answer,
      but the mouths of wicked people pour out
        a flood of evil things.

<sup>29</sup> The LORD is far from wicked people,
      but he hears the prayers of righteous people.

<sup>30</sup> A twinkle in the eye delights the heart.
      Good news refreshes the body.

<sup>31</sup> The ear that listens to a life-giving warning
      will be at home among wise people.

<sup>32</sup> Whoever ignores discipline despises himself,
      but the person who listens to warning
        gains understanding.

<sup>33</sup> The fear of the LORD is discipline ˌleading
    toˌ wisdom,
      and humility comes before honor.

# *Day 44* ≈

## PSALM 77

For the choir director; according to Jeduthun;
a psalm by Asaph.

<sup>1</sup> Loudly, I cried to God.
    Loudly, I cried to God
      so that he would open his ears to ˌhearˌ me.

2  On the day I was in trouble, I went to the Lord
        for help.
    At night I stretched out my hands in prayer
        without growing tired.
        Yet, my soul refused to be comforted.

3  I sigh as I remember God.
    I begin to lose hope as I think about him.          *Selah*
4      (You keep my eyelids open.)
    I am so upset that I cannot speak.
5  I have considered the days of old,
        the years long ago.
6  I remember my song in the night
        and reflect ͺon itͺ.
    My spirit searches ͺfor an answerͺ:
7      Will the Lord reject ͺmeͺ for all time?
        Will he ever accept me?
8      Has his mercy come to an end forever?
        Has his promise been canceled
            throughout every generation?
9      Has God forgotten to be merciful?
        Has he locked up his compassion
            because of his anger?                       *Selah*
10         Then I said, "It makes me feel sick
            that the power of the Most High
                is no longer the same."[a]

11 I will remember the deeds of the LORD.
    I will remember your ancient miracles.
12 I will reflect on all your actions
        and think about what you have done.

---

[a] 77:10 Hebrew meaning of this line uncertain.

<sup>13</sup> O God, your ways are holy!
    What god is as great as our God?
<sup>14</sup> You are the God who performs miracles.
    You have made your strength known
        among the nations.
<sup>15</sup> With your might you have defended your people,
    the descendants of Jacob and Joseph.    *Selah*

<sup>16</sup> The water saw you, O God.
    The water saw you and shook.
        Even the depths of the sea trembled.
<sup>17</sup> The clouds poured out water.
    The sky thundered.
        Even your arrows flashed in every direction.
<sup>18</sup> The sound of your thunder rumbled in the sky.[a]
    Streaks of lightning lit up the world.
        The earth trembled and shook.

<sup>19</sup> Your road went through the sea.
    Your path went through raging water,
        but your footprints could not be seen.
<sup>20</sup> Like a shepherd, you led your people.
    You had Moses and Aaron take them by the hand.

## PROVERBS 16:1-9

### Wisdom's Blessings Come From the LORD

<sup>1</sup> The plans of the heart belong to humans,
    but an answer on the tongue comes
        from the LORD.
<sup>2</sup> A person thinks all his ways are pure,
    but the LORD weighs motives.

---

[a] 77:18 Hebrew meaning of this line uncertain.

³ Entrust your efforts to the LORD,
    and your plans will succeed.
⁴ The LORD has made everything for his own purpose,
    even wicked people for the day of trouble.
⁵ Everyone with a conceited heart is disgusting
      to the LORD.
    Certainly, ⌐such a person⌐ will not go unpunished.

⁶ By mercy and faithfulness, peace is made
      with the LORD.
    By the fear of the LORD, evil is avoided.
⁷ When a person's ways are pleasing to the LORD,
    he makes even his enemies to be at peace
      with him.
⁸ Better a few ⌐possessions⌐ gained honestly
    than many gained through injustice.
⁹ A person may plan his own journey,
    but the LORD directs his steps.

# Day 45 ⁓

## PSALM 78:1-39

A *maskil* by Asaph.

¹ Open your ears to my teachings, my people.
    Turn your ears to the words from my mouth.
²   I will open my mouth to illustrate points.
    I will explain what has been hidden long ago,
³     things that we have heard and known about,
      things that our parents have told us.

4     We will not hide them from our children.
We will tell the next generation
about the LORD's power and great deeds
and the miraculous things he has done.

5   He established written instructions
for Jacob's people.
He gave his teachings to Israel.
He commanded our ancestors to make them known
to their children
6     so that the next generation would know them.
Children yet to be born ⌊would learn them⌋.
They will grow up and tell their children
7     to trust God, to remember what he has done,
and to obey his commands.
8     Then they will not be like their ancestors,
a stubborn and rebellious generation.
Their hearts were not loyal.
Their spirits were not faithful to God.

9   The men of Ephraim, well-equipped
with bows ⌊and arrows⌋,
turned ⌊and ran⌋ on the day of battle.
10     They had not been faithful to God's promise.[a]
They refused to follow his teachings.
11     They forgot what he had done—
the miracles that he had shown them.

12   In front of their ancestors he performed miracles
in the land of Egypt, in the fields of Zoan.
13     He divided the sea and led them through it.
He made the waters stand up like a wall.

---

[a] 78:10 Or "covenant."

¹⁴        He guided them by a cloud during the day
          and by a fiery light throughout the night.
¹⁵        He split rocks in the desert.
       He gave them plenty to drink,
          an ocean of water.
¹⁶        He made streams come out of a rock.
       He made the water flow like rivers.

¹⁷ They continued to sin against him,
    to rebel in the desert against the Most High.
¹⁸ They deliberately tested God by demanding
    the food they craved.
¹⁹ They spoke against God by saying,
    "Can God prepare a banquet in the desert?
²⁰ True, he did strike a rock,
    and water did gush out,
        and the streams did overflow.
    But can he also give us bread or provide us,
        his people, with meat?"

²¹ When the Lord heard this, he became furious.
    His fire burned against Jacob
        and his anger flared up at Israel
²²            because they did not believe God
             or trust him to save them.

²³ In spite of that, he commanded the clouds above
    and opened the doors of heaven.
²⁴         He rained manna down on them to eat
          and gave them grain from heaven.
²⁵         Humans ate the bread of the mighty ones,
          and God sent them plenty of food.

²⁶ He made the east wind blow in the heavens
    and guided the south wind with his might.

27         He rained meat down on them like dust,
            birds like the sand on the seashore.
28            He made the birds fall in the middle
                of his camp,
          all around his dwelling place.

29    They ate more than enough.
       He gave them what they wanted,
30            but they still wanted more.
           While the food was still in their mouths,
31              the anger of God flared up against them.
          He killed their strongest men
             and slaughtered the best young men
                in Israel.

32   In spite of all this, they continued to sin,
     and they no longer believed in his miracles.
33           He brought their days to an end like a whisper
             in the wind.
          He brought their years to an end in terror.
34           When he killed ⌊some of⌋ them,
            ⌊the rest⌋ searched for him.
          They turned from their sins
            and eagerly looked for God.
35           They remembered that God was their rock,
            that the Most High was their defender.
36           They flattered him with their mouths
            and lied to him with their tongues.
37           Their hearts were not loyal to him.
          They were not faithful to his promise.

38   But he is compassionate.
       He forgave their sin.
          He did not destroy them.

He restrained his anger many times.
He did not display all of his fury.

<sup>39</sup> He remembered
that they were only flesh and blood,
a breeze that blows and does not return.

## PROVERBS 16:10-19

<sup>10</sup> When a divine revelation is on a king's lips,
he cannot voice a wrong judgment.

<sup>11</sup> Honest balances and scales belong to the LORD.
He made the entire set of weights.

<sup>12</sup> Wrongdoing is disgusting to kings
because a throne is established
through righteousness.

<sup>13</sup> Kings are happy with honest words,
and whoever speaks what is right is loved.

<sup>14</sup> A king's anger announces death,
but a wise man makes peace with him.

<sup>15</sup> When the king is cheerful, there is life,
and his favor is like a cloud bringing spring rain.

<sup>16</sup> How much better it is to gain wisdom than gold,
and the gaining of understanding
should be chosen over silver.

<sup>17</sup> The highway of decent people turns away from evil.
Whoever watches his way preserves his own life.

<sup>18</sup> Pride precedes a disaster,
and an arrogant attitude precedes a fall.

<sup>19</sup> Better to be humble with lowly people
than to share stolen goods with arrogant people.

# Day 46 ≈

## PSALM 78:40-72

40   How often they rebelled against him
     in the wilderness!
How often they caused him grief in the desert!

41   Again and again they tested God,
     and they pushed the Holy One of Israel
       to the limit.

42   They did not remember his power—
     the day he freed them from their oppressor,

43      when he performed his miraculous signs
       in Egypt,
     his wonders in the fields of Zoan.

44   He turned their rivers into blood
     so that they could not drink from their streams.

45   He sent a swarm of flies that bit them
     and frogs that ruined them.

46   He gave their crops to grasshoppers
     and their produce to locusts.

47   He killed their vines with hail
     and their fig trees with frost.

48   He let the hail strike their cattle
     and bolts of lightning strike their livestock.

49   He sent his burning anger, rage, fury,
     and hostility against them.
He sent an army of destroying angels.

50   He cleared a path for his anger.
He did not spare them.
He let the plague take their lives.

51 He slaughtered every firstborn in Egypt,
    the ones born in the tents of Ham
        when their fathers were young.

52 But he led his own people out like sheep
    and guided them like a flock
        through the wilderness.
53     He led them safely.
        They had no fear while the sea
           covered their enemies.
54 He brought them into his holy land,
    to this mountain that his power had won.
55     He forced nations out of their way
        and gave them the land of the nations
           as their inheritance.
        He settled the tribes of Israel
           in their own tents.

56 They tested God Most High and rebelled against him.
    They did not obey his written instructions.
57 They were disloyal and treacherous
    like their ancestors.
    They were like arrows shot from a defective bow.
58 They made him angry
    because of their illegal worship sites.
    They made him furious
    because they worshiped idols.

59 When God heard, he became furious.
    He completely rejected Israel.
60     He abandoned his dwelling place in Shiloh,
        the tent where he had lived among humans.
61     He allowed his power to be taken captive
        and handed his glory over to an oppressor.

62    He let swords kill his people.
       He was furious with those who belonged to him.
63        Fire consumed his best young men,
              so his virgins heard no wedding songs.
64        His priests were cut down with swords.
           The widows ˏof his priests˩
               could not even weep ˏfor them˩.
65    Then the Lord woke up
           like one who had been sleeping,
         like a warrior sobering up from ˏtoo much˩ wine.
66    He struck his enemies from behind
         and disgraced them forever.

67    He rejected the tent of Joseph.
       He did not choose the tribe of Ephraim,
68        but he chose the tribe of Judah,
           Mount Zion which he loved.
69    He built his holy place to be like the high heavens,
         like the earth which he made to last
             for a long time.

70    He chose his servant David.
       He took him from the sheep pens.
71    He brought him from tending the ewes
             that had lambs
         so that David could be the shepherd
             of the people of Jacob,
             of Israel, the people who belonged to the LORD.
72    With unselfish devotion David became their shepherd.
       With skill he guided them.

### PROVERBS 16:20-33

20    Whoever gives attention
           to the LORD's word prospers,

and blessed is the person who trusts the LORD.

21 The person who is truly wise is called understanding,
and speaking sweetly helps others learn.

22 Understanding is a fountain of life to the one
who has it,
but stubborn fools punish themselves
with their stupidity.

23 A wise person's heart controls his speech,
and what he says helps others learn.

24 Pleasant words are like honey from a honeycomb—
sweet to the spirit and healthy for the body.

## Words of Advice to a Wise Son

25 There is a way that seems right to a person,
but eventually it ends in death.

26 A laborer's appetite works to his advantage,
because his hunger drives him on.

27 A worthless person plots trouble,
and his speech is like a burning fire.

28 A devious person spreads quarrels.
A gossip separates the closest of friends.

29 A violent person misleads his neighbor
and leads him on a path that is not good.

30 Whoever winks his eye is plotting
something devious.
Whoever bites his lips has finished his evil work.

31 Silver hair is a beautiful crown found
in a righteous life.

32 Better to get angry slowly than to be a hero.
Better to be even-tempered than to capture a city.

33 The dice are thrown,
but the LORD determines every outcome.

# Day 47 ➴

## PSALM 79

A psalm by Asaph.

1     O God, the nations have invaded the land
       that belongs to you.
    They have dishonored your holy temple.
    They have left Jerusalem in ruins.

2     They have given the dead bodies of your servants
       to the birds for food.
    They have given the flesh of your godly ones
       to the animals.

3     They have shed the blood of your people
       around Jerusalem
       as though it were water.
       There is no one to bury your people.

4     We have become a disgrace to our neighbors,
       an object of ridicule and contempt
       to those around us.

5     How long, O LORD?
    Will you remain angry forever?
    Will your fury continue to burn like fire?

6     Pour your fury on the nations that do not know you,
       on the kingdoms that have not called you.

7        They have devoured Jacob.
       They have destroyed his home.

8     Do not hold the crimes of our ancestors against us.
    Reach out to us soon with your compassion,
       because we are helpless.

⁹  Help us, O God, our savior, for the glory
        of your name.
    Rescue us, and forgive our sins for the honor
        of your name.

¹⁰ Why should the nations ⌊be allowed to⌋ s a y,
        "Where is their God?"
    Let us watch as the nations learn
        that there is punishment for shedding the blood
            of your servants.
¹¹ Let the groans of prisoners
        come into your presence.
    With your powerful arm rescue those
        who are condemned to death.
¹² Pay each one of our neighbors back
        with seven times the number of insults
            they used to insult you, O Lord.
¹³ Then we, your people, the flock in your pasture,
        will give thanks to you forever.
        We will praise you throughout every generation.


## PSALM 80

For the choir director; according to *shoshannim eduth*;
by Asaph; a psalm.

¹  Open your ears, O Shepherd of Israel,
        the one who leads ⌊the descendants of⌋ Joseph
            like sheep,
        the one who is enthroned over the angels.*
²  Appear in front of Ephraim, Benjamin,
        and Manasseh.
    Wake up your power, and come to save us.

---

* 80:1 Or "cherubim."

³   O God, restore us and smile on us
    so that we may be saved.

⁴   O LORD God, commander of armies,
    how long will you smolder in anger
  against the prayer of your people?
⁵   You made them eat tears as food.
  You often made them drink ˻their own˼ tears.
⁶   You made us a source of conflict to our neighbors,
  and our enemies made fun of us.

⁷   O God, commander of armies, restore us
    and smile on us
    so that we may be saved.

⁸   You brought a vine from Egypt.
  You forced out the nations and planted it.
⁹   You cleared the ground for it
    so that it took root and filled the land.
¹⁰       Its shade covered the mountains.
    Its branches covered the mighty cedars.
¹¹       It reached out with its branches
      to the Mediterranean Sea.
    Its shoots reached the Euphrates River.

¹²   Why did you break down the stone fences
    around this vine?
  All who pass by are picking its fruit.
¹³       Wild boars from the forest graze on it.
    Wild animals devour it.
¹⁴   O God, commander of armies, come back!
  Look from heaven and see!
  Come to help this vine.
¹⁵   Take care of what your right hand planted,
  the son you strengthened for yourself.

16    The vine has been cut down and burned.
          Let them be destroyed
                by the threatening look on your face.

17   Let your power rest on the man you have chosen,
          the son of man you strengthened for yourself.
18          Then we will never turn away from you.
                Give us life again, and we will call on you.

19   O LORD God, commander of armies, restore us,
          and smile on us
          so that we may be saved.


## PROVERBS 17:1-6

1    Better a bite of dry bread ˛eaten� in peace
          than a family feast filled with strife.
2    A wise slave will become master over a son
              who acts shamefully,
          and he will share the inheritance
              with the brothers.
3    The crucible is for refining silver and the smelter
              for gold,
          but the one who purifies hearts ˛by fire�
              is the LORD.
4    An evildoer pays attention to wicked lips.
     A liar opens his ears to a slanderous tongue.
5          Whoever makes fun of a poor person insults
              his maker.
          Whoever is happy ˛to see someone's� distress
              will not escape punishment.
6    Grandchildren are the crown of grandparents,
          and parents are the glory of their children.

# *Day 48* ➳

## PSALM 81

For the choir director; on the *gittith;*[a] by Asaph.

1   Sing joyfully to God, our strength.
    Shout happily to the God of Jacob.
2   Begin a psalm, and strike a tambourine.
    Play lyres and harps with their pleasant music.
3   Blow the ram's horn on the day of the new moon,
      on the day of the full moon,
      on our festival days.
4   This is a law for Israel,
      a legal decision from the God of Jacob.
5       These are the instructions God set in place
        for Joseph
        when Joseph rose to power over Egypt.

    I heard a message I did not understand:
6   "I removed the burden from his shoulder.
      His hands were freed from the basket.
7   When you were in trouble, you called out ⸤to me⸥,
      and I rescued you.
    I was hidden in thunder, but I answered you.
    I tested your ⸤loyalty⸥ at the oasis of Meribah. *Selah*
8       Listen, my people, and I will warn you.
        Israel, if you would only listen to me!
9       Never keep any strange god among you.
        Never worship a foreign god.

---

[a] 81:1 Unknown musical term.

10    I am the LORD your God, the one
           who brought you out of Egypt.
           Open your mouth wide, and I will fill it.

11    "But my people did not listen to me.
           Israel wanted nothing to do with me.
12         So I let them go their own stubborn ways
           and follow their own advice.
13    If only my people would listen to me!
      If only Israel would follow me!
14         I would quickly defeat their enemies.
      I would turn my power against their foes.
15         Those who hate the LORD would cringe
                in front of him,
           and their time ⸢for punishment⸥
                would last forever.
16    But I would feed Israel with the finest wheat
           and satisfy them with honey from a rock."

## PSALM 82

A psalm by Asaph.

1    God takes his place in his own assembly.
      He pronounces judgment among the gods:
2         "How long are you going to judge unfairly?
      How long are you going to side
                with wicked people?"                    *Selah*

3    Defend weak people and orphans.
      Protect the rights of the oppressed and the poor.
4    Rescue weak and needy people.
           Help them escape the power of wicked people.

5    Wicked people do not know or understand anything.
           As they walk around in the dark,

all the foundations of the earth shake.
⁶ I said, "You are gods.
    You are all sons of the Most High.
⁷        You will certainly die like humans
            and fall like any prince."

⁸ Arise, O God!
    Judge the earth, because all the nations
        belong to you.

## PROVERBS 17:7-15

### The Consequences of Being a Fool

⁷ Refined speech is not fitting for a godless fool.
    How much less does lying fit a noble person!
⁸ A bribe seems ⸤like⸥ a jewel to the one who gives it.ᵃ
    Wherever he turns, he prospers.
⁹ Whoever forgives an offense seeks love,
    but whoever keeps bringing up the issue
        separates the closest of friends.

¹⁰ A reprimand impresses a person
        who has understanding
    more than a hundred lashes impress a fool.
¹¹ A rebel looks for nothing but evil.
    Therefore, a cruel messenger will be sent
        ⸤to punish⸥ him.
¹² Better to meet a bear robbed of its cubs
    than a fool ⸤carried away⸥ with his stupidity.
¹³ Whoever pays back evil for good—
    evil will never leave his home.
¹⁴ Starting a quarrel is ⸤like⸥ opening a floodgate,
    so stop before the argument gets out of control.

─────────────────
ᵃ 17:8 Or "who receives it."

15    Whoever approves of wicked people
           and whoever condemns righteous people
              is disgusting to the LORD.


# Day 49 ⁓

## PSALM 83

A song; a psalm by Asaph.

1    O God, do not remain silent.
           Do not turn a deaf ear to me.
           Do not keep quiet, O God.

2    Look, your enemies are in an uproar.
           Those who hate you hold their heads high.
3              They make plans in secret against your people
                  and plot together against those you treasure.
4              They say, "Let's wipe out their nation
                  so that the name of Israel will no longer
                     be remembered."
5              They agree completely on their plan.
                  They form an alliance against you:
6                  the tents from Edom and Ishmael,
                     Moab and Hagar,
7                  Gebal, Ammon, and Amalek,
                     Philistia, along with those who live in Tyre.
8                  Even Assyria has joined them.
                     They helped the descendants of Lot. *Selah*
9    Do to them what you did to Midian,
           to Sisera and Jabin at the Kishon River.
10             They were destroyed at Endor.
                  They became manure to fertilize the ground.

11     Treat their influential people as you treated
          Oreb and Zeeb.
     Treat all their leaders like Zebah and Zalmunna.
12       They said, "Let's take God's pasturelands
           for ourselves."
13     O my God, blow them away like tumbleweeds,[a]
     like husks in the wind.
14     Pursue them with your storms,
     and terrify them with your windstorms
15       the way fire burns a forest
        and flames set mountains on fire.[b]
16     Let their faces blush with shame, O LORD,
     so that they must look to you for help.
17     Let them be put to shame and terrified forever.
     Let them die in disgrace
18       so that they must acknowledge you.
        Your name is the LORD.
        You alone are the Most High God
          of the whole earth.

## PSALM 84

For the choir director; on the *gittith*;
a psalm by Korah's descendants.

1     Your dwelling place is lovely, O LORD of Armies!
2       My soul longs and yearns
        for the LORD's courtyards.
      My whole body shouts for joy to the living God.
3        Even sparrows find a home,
         and swallows find a nest for themselves.
        There they hatch their young

---

[a] 83:13 Or "whirling dust."   [b] 83:15 Verse 15 (in Hebrew) has been placed in front of verse 14 to express the complex Hebrew sentence structure more clearly in English.

near your altars, O LORD of Armies,
my king and my God.
⁴ Blessed are those who live in your house.
They are always praising you.            *Selah*

⁵ Blessed are those who find strength in you.
Their hearts are on the road ⸢that leads to you⸥.ᵃ
⁶        As they pass through a valley
where balsam trees grow,ᵇ
they make it a place of springs.
The early rains cover it with blessings.ᶜ
⁷            Their strength grows as they go along
until each one of them appears
in front of God in Zion.

⁸ O LORD God, commander of armies, hear my prayer.
Open your ears, O God of Jacob.            *Selah*
⁹    Look at our shield, O God.
Look with favor on the face of your anointed one.
¹⁰ One day in your courtyards is better
than a thousand ⸢anywhere else⸥.
I would rather stand in the entrance
to my God's house
than live inside wicked people's homes.
¹¹ The LORD God is a sun and shield.
The LORD grants favor and honor.
He does not hold back any blessing
from those who live innocently.

¹² O LORD of Armies, blessed is the person
who trusts you.

---

ᵃ 84:5 Hebrew meaning of this line uncertain.   ᵇ 84:6 Or "As they pass through the valley of Weeping."
ᶜ 84:6 Or "pools."

## PROVERBS 17:16-28

16   Why should a fool have money in his hand
         to buy wisdom
         when he doesn't have a mind to grasp anything?
17   A friend always loves,
         and a brother is born to share trouble.
18   A person without good sense closes a deal
         with a handshake.
      He guarantees a loan in the presence
         of his friend.
19   Whoever loves sin loves a quarrel.
      Whoever builds his city gate high invites destruction.
20      A twisted mind never finds happiness,
            and one with a devious tongue ⌊repeatedly⌋
               gets into trouble.
21   The parent of a fool has grief,
         and the father of a godless fool has no joy.
22   A joyful heart is good medicine,
         but depression drains one's strength.
23   A wicked person secretly accepts a bribe
         to corrupt the ways of justice.
24   Wisdom is directly in front
         of an understanding person,
      but the eyes of a fool ⌊are looking around⌋
         all over the world.

### How Fools Live

25   A foolish son is a heartache to his father
         and bitter grief to his mother.

26   To punish an innocent person is not good.
      To strike down noble people is not right.

<sup>27</sup>     Whoever has knowledge controls his words,
          and a person who has understanding
              is even-tempered.

<sup>28</sup>    Even a stubborn fool is thought to be wise
          if he keeps silent.
      He is considered intelligent
          if he keeps his lips sealed.

# *Day 50* &#x7E;

## PSALM 85

For the choir director; a psalm by Korah's descendants.

<sup>1</sup>    You favored your land, O LORD.
     You restored the fortunes of Jacob.
<sup>2</sup>    You removed your people's guilt.
     You pardoned all their sins.                     *Selah*
<sup>3</sup>    You laid aside all your fury.
     You turned away from your burning anger.

<sup>4</sup>    Restore us, O God, our savior.
     Put an end to your anger against us.
<sup>5</sup>       Will you be angry with us forever?
         Will you ever let go of your anger
              in the generations to come?
<sup>6</sup>       Won't you restore our lives again
              so that your people may find joy in you?
<sup>7</sup>          Show us your mercy, O LORD,
                 by giving us your salvation.

8    I want to hear what God the LORD says,
        because he promises peace to his people,
            to his godly ones.
            But they must not go back to their stupidity.
9    Indeed, his salvation is near those who fear him,
        and ˌhisˌ glory will remain in our land.

10   Mercy and truth have met.
     Righteousness and peace have kissed.
11   Truth sprouts from the ground,
        and righteousness looks down from heaven.
12   The LORD will certainly give us what is good,
        and our land will produce crops.
13   Righteousness will go ahead of him
        and make a path for his steps.


## PSALM 86

A prayer by David.

1    Turn your ear ˌtoward meˌ, O LORD.
     Answer me, because I am oppressed and needy.
2    Protect me, because I am faithful ˌto youˌ.
     Save your servant who trusts you. You are my God.
3    Have pity on me, O Lord,
        because I call out to you all day long.
4    Give me joy, O Lord,
        because I lift my soul to you.
5    You, O Lord, are good and forgiving,
        full of mercy toward everyone
            who calls out to you.
6    Open your ears to my prayer, O LORD.
     Pay attention when I plead for mercy.

7    When I am in trouble, I call out to you
         because you answer me.

8    No god is like you, O Lord.
     No one can do what you do.
9    All the nations that you have made
         will bow in your presence, O Lord.
             They will honor you.
10   Indeed, you are great, a worker of miracles.
         You alone are God.
11   Teach me your way, O LORD,
         so that I may live in your truth.
     Focus my heart on fearing you.
12   I will give thanks to you with all my heart,
             O Lord my God.
     I will honor you forever
13       because your mercy toward me is great.
             You have rescued me from the depths of hell.

14   O God, arrogant people attack me,
         and a mob of ruthless people seeks my life.
             They think nothing of you.
15   But you, O Lord, are a compassionate
             and merciful God.
         You are patient, always faithful
             and ready to forgive.
16   Turn toward me, and have pity on me.
     Give me your strength because I am your servant.
     Save me because I am the son
         of your female servant.
17   Grant me some proof of your goodness
         so that those who hate me may see it
             and be put to shame.
     You, O LORD, have helped me and comforted me.

## PROVERBS 18:1-8

1  A loner is out to get what he wants for himself.
    He opposes all sound reasoning.

2  A fool does not find joy in understanding
      but only in expressing his own opinion.

3  When wickedness comes, contempt also comes,
      and insult comes along with disgrace.

4  The words of a person's mouth are like deep waters.
    The fountain of wisdom is an overflowing stream.

5  It is not good to be partial toward a wicked person,
      thereby depriving an innocent person of justice.

6  By talking, a fool gets into an argument,
      and his mouth invites a beating.

7  A fool's mouth is his ruin.
    His lips are a trap to his soul.

8  The words of a gossip are swallowed greedily,
      and they go down
          into a person's innermost being.

# *Day 51* ≈

## PSALM 87

By Korah's descendants; a psalm; a song.

1  ‚The city‚ the Lord has founded ‚stands‚
      on holy mountains.

2  The Lord loves the city of Zion
      more than any other place in Jacob.

3  Glorious things are said about you, O city of God!
                         *Selah*

<sup>4</sup> The LORD says, "I will add Egypt and Babylon
  as well as Philistia, Tyre, and Sudan
   to the list of those who acknowledge me.
   Each nation will claim that it
    was born there."

<sup>5</sup> But it will be said of Zion,
  "Every race is born in it.
   The Most High will make it secure."
<sup>6</sup> The LORD will record this in the Book of Nations:
  "Every race claims that it was born there." *Selah*
<sup>7</sup> Singers and dancers will sing,
  "Zion is the source of all our blessings."

## PSALM 88

A song; a psalm by Korah's descendants; for the choir
director; according to *mahalath leannoth*;<sup>a</sup> a *maskil* by
Heman the Ezrahite.

<sup>1</sup> O LORD God, my savior,
  I cry out to you during the day and at night.
<sup>2</sup>   Let my prayer come into your presence.
   Turn your ear to hear my cries.
<sup>3</sup> My soul is filled with troubles,
  and my life comes closer to the grave.
<sup>4</sup>   I am numbered with those who go into the pit.
  I am like a man without any strength—
<sup>5</sup>    abandoned with the dead,
   like those who have been killed
    and lie in graves,
   like those whom you no longer remember,
    who are cut off from your power.

---

<sup>a</sup> 88:1 Unknown musical term.

⁶ You have put me in the bottom of the pit—
        in deep, dark places.
⁷ Your rage lies heavily on me.
    You make all your waves pound on me.        *Selah*
⁸ You have taken my friends far away from me.
    You made me disgusting to them.
        I'm shut in, and I can't get out.
⁹        My eyes grow weak because of my suffering.
            All day long I call out to you, O LORD.
                I stretch out my hands to you ⌊in prayer⌋.

¹⁰ Will you perform miracles for those who are dead?
    Will the spirits of the dead rise and give thanks
        to you?                                *Selah*
¹¹ Will anyone tell about your mercy in Sheol
        or about your faithfulness in Abaddon?
¹² Will anyone know about your miracles
        in that dark place
        or about your righteousness in the place
            where forgotten people live?

¹³ I cry out to you for help, O LORD,
        and in the morning my prayer will come
            into your presence.

¹⁴ Why do you reject my soul, O LORD?
    Why do you hide your face from me?
¹⁵        Ever since I was young, I have been suffering
            and near death.
        I have endured your terrors, and now
            I am in despair.ᵃ

---

ᵃ 88:15 Hebrew meaning uncertain.

16 Your burning anger has swept over me.
Your terrors have destroyed me.
17 They swirl around me all day long like water.
They surround me on all sides.
18 You have taken my loved ones and friends
far away from me.
Darkness is my only friend![a]

## PROVERBS 18:9-16

### How to Avoid Fools and Foolishness

9 Whoever is lazy in his work is related to a vandal.
10 The name of the LORD is a strong tower.
A righteous person runs to it and is safe.
11 A rich person's wealth is his strong city
and is like a high wall in his imagination.

12 Before destruction a person's heart is arrogant,
but humility comes before honor.
13 Whoever gives an answer before he listens
is stupid and shameful.
14 A person's spirit can endure sickness,
but who can bear a broken spirit?
15 The mind of a person who has understanding
acquires knowledge.
The ears of wise people seek knowledge.
16 A gift opens doors for the one who gives it
and brings him into the presence of great people.

---

[a] 88:18 Hebrew meaning uncertain.

# *Day 52* ≈

## PSALM 89

A *maskil* by Ethan the Ezrahite.

1   I will sing forever about the evidence of your mercy,
       O LORD.
   I will tell about your faithfulness to every generation.

2   I said, "Your mercy will last forever.
       Your faithfulness stands firm in the heavens."

3   ⸤You said,⸥ "I have made a promise*a*
       to my chosen one.
   I swore this oath to my servant David:

4       'I will make your dynasty continue forever.
       I built your throne to last
           throughout every generation.' "      *Selah*

5   O LORD, the heavens praise your miracles
       and your faithfulness in the assembly
          of the holy ones.

6   Who in the skies can compare with the LORD?
   Who among the heavenly beings is like the LORD?

7   God is terrifying in the council of the holy ones.
   He is greater and more awe-inspiring than those
       who surround him.

8   O LORD God of Armies, who is like you?
   Mighty LORD, even your faithfulness surrounds you.

9       You rule the raging sea.
       When its waves rise, you quiet them.

---

*a* 89:3 Or "covenant."

<sup>10</sup>       You crushed Rahab;<sup>a</sup> it was like a corpse.
          With your strong arm you scattered your enemies.
<sup>11</sup>   The heavens are yours.
      The earth is also yours.
      You made the world and everything in it.
<sup>12</sup>       You created north and south.
              Mount Tabor and Mount Hermon
                      sing your name joyfully.
<sup>13</sup>       Your arm is mighty.
          Your hand is strong.
          Your right hand is lifted high.
<sup>14</sup>   Righteousness and justice are the foundations
              of your throne.
      Mercy and truth stand in front of you.
<sup>15</sup>   Blessed are the people who know how to praise you.
          They walk in the light of your presence, O Lord.
<sup>16</sup>       They find joy in your name all day long.
          They are joyful in your righteousness
<sup>17</sup>           because you are the glory of their strength.
      By your favor you give us victory.<sup>b</sup>
<sup>18</sup>   Our shield belongs to the Lord.
      Our king belongs to the Holy One of Israel.

<sup>19</sup>   Once in a vision you said to your faithful ones:
          "I set a boy above warriors.<sup>c</sup>
          I have raised up one chosen from the people.
<sup>20</sup>       I found my servant David.
          I anointed him with my holy oil.
<sup>21</sup>           My hand is ready to help him.
              My arm will also give him strength.

---

<sup>a</sup> 89:10 Rahab is the name of a demonic creature who opposes God.   <sup>b</sup> 89:17 Hebrew meaning of
"give us victory" uncertain.   <sup>c</sup> 89:19 Hebrew meaning of this line uncertain.

22      No enemy will take him by surprise.
         No wicked person will mistreat him.

23    I will crush his enemies in front of him
       and defeat those who hate him.

24    My faithfulness and mercy will be with him,
       and in my name he will be victorious.[a]

25    I will put his ⌊left⌋ hand on the sea
       and his right hand on the rivers.

26    He will call out to me,
       'You are my Father, my God, and the rock
         of my salvation.'

27    Yes, I will make him the firstborn.
       He will be the Most High to the kings
         of the earth.

28    My mercy will stay with him forever.
       My promise to him is unbreakable.

29    I will make his dynasty endure forever
       and his throne like the days of heaven.

30    "If his descendants abandon my teachings
       and do not live by my rules,

31    if they violate my laws
       and do not obey my commandments,

32    then with a rod I will punish their rebellion
       and their crimes with beatings.

33    But I will not take my mercy away from him
       or allow my truth to become a lie.

34    I will not dishonor my promise
       or alter my own agreement.

35    On my holiness I have taken an oath once
         and for all:
       I will not lie to David.

---

[a] 89:24 Hebrew meaning of "he will be victorious" uncertain.

³⁶ His dynasty will last forever.
  His throne will be in my presence like the sun.
³⁷ Like the moon his throne
  will stand firm forever.
  It will be like a faithful witness in heaven."

³⁸ But you have despised, rejected,
  and become angry with your anointed one.
³⁹ You have refused to recognize the promise
  to your servant
  and have thrown his crown into the dirt.
⁴⁰ You have broken through all his walls
  and have laid his fortified cities in ruins.
⁴¹ (Everyone who passed by robbed him.
  He has become the object
  of his neighbors' scorn.)
⁴² You held the right hand of his enemies high
  and made all of his adversaries rejoice.
⁴³ You even took his sword out of his hand
  and failed to support him in battle.
⁴⁴ You put an end to his splendor
  and hurled his throne to the ground.
⁴⁵ You cut short the days of his youth
  and covered him with shame.          *Selah*

⁴⁶ How long, O LORD? Will you hide yourself forever?
  How long will your anger continue to burn like fire?
⁴⁷ Remember how short my life is!
  Have you created Adam's descendants
  for no reason?
⁴⁸ Can a mortal go on living and never see death?
  Who can set himself free from the power
  of the grave?          *Selah*
⁴⁹ Where is the evidence of your mercy, Lord?

You swore an oath to David
on the basis of your faithfulness.

50    Remember, O LORD,[a]
          how your servant[b] has been insulted.
      Remember how I have carried in my heart
          the insults from so many people.
51        Your enemies insulted me.
              They insulted your Messiah[c] every step he took.

52                Thank the LORD forever.
                    Amen and amen!

## PROVERBS 18:17-24

17    The first to state his case seems right
          until his neighbor comes to cross-examine him.
18    Flipping a coin ends quarrels
          and settles issues between powerful people.
19    An offended brother is more resistant
              than a strong city,
          and disputes are like the locked gate
              of a castle tower.

20    A person's speaking ability provides for his stomach.
      His talking provides him a living.
21    The tongue has the power of life and death,
          and those who love to talk will have to eat
              their own words.

22    Whoever finds a wife finds something good
          and has obtained favor from the LORD.

---

*a* 89:50 Many Hebrew manuscripts; other Hebrew manuscripts "Lord."    *b* 89:50 Many Hebrew
manuscripts, Greek, Syriac; other Hebrew manuscripts "your servants."    *c* 89:51 Or "anointed one."

23 A poor person is timid when begging,
   but a rich person is blunt when replying.
24 Friends can destroy one another,[a]
   but a loving friend can stick closer than family.

# Day 53 ❧

## PSALM 90

A prayer by Moses, the man of God.

1 O Lord, you have been our refuge
   throughout every generation.
2 Before the mountains were born,
   before you gave birth to the earth and the world,
      you were God.
   You are God from everlasting to everlasting.

3 You turn mortals back into dust
   and say, "Return, descendants of Adam."
4 Indeed, in your sight a thousand years
      are like a single day,
   like yesterday—already past—
   like an hour in the night.
5 You sweep mortals away.
   They are a dream.
   They sprout again in the morning like cut grass.
6    In the morning they blossom and sprout.
     In the evening they wither and dry up.

7 Indeed, your anger consumes us.
   Your rage terrifies us.

---
[a] 18:24 Or "A person has friends as companions."

8       You have set our sins in front of you.
        You have put our secret sins in the light
            of your presence.
9   Indeed, all our days slip away because of your fury.
        We live out our years like one ˌlongˌ sigh.
10  Each of us lives for 70 years—
        or even 80 if we are in good health.
            But the best of them[a]
                ˌbringˌ trouble and misery.
            Indeed, they are soon gone,
                and we fly away.
11  Who fully understands the power of your anger?
        A person fears you more when he better
            understands your fury.[b]
12  Teach us to number each of our days
        so that we may grow in wisdom.

13  Return, LORD! How long. . . ?
        Change your plans about ˌus,ˌ your servants.
14  Satisfy us every morning with your mercy
        so that we may sing joyfully and rejoice
            all our days.
15  Make us rejoice for as many days
        as you have made us suffer,
            for as many years as we have experienced evil.
16  Let ˌus,ˌ your servants, see what you can do.
        Let our children see your glorious power.
17  Let the kindness of the Lord our God be with us.
        Make us successful in everything we do.
            Yes, make us successful in everything we do.

---

[a] 90:10 Hebrew meaning of "the best of them" uncertain.   [b] 90:11 Hebrew meaning of this
line uncertain.

## PSALM 91

¹ Whoever lives under the shelter of the Most High
   will remain in the shadow of the Almighty.
² I will say to the LORD,
      "You are my refuge and my fortress,
         my God in whom I trust."

³ He is the one who will rescue you from hunters' traps
   and from deadly plagues.
⁴ He will cover you with his feathers,
      and under his wings you will find refuge.
         His truth is your shield and armor.

⁵ You do not need to fear
      terrors of the night,
      arrows that fly during the day,
⁶   plagues that roam the dark,
      epidemics that strike at noon.
⁷      They will not come near you,
            even though a thousand may fall dead
               beside you
            or ten thousand at your right side.

⁸ You only have to look with your eyes
   to see the punishment of wicked people.

⁹ You, O LORD, are my refuge!

You have made the Most High your home.
¹⁰     No harm will come to you.
      No sickness will come near your house.
¹¹ He will put his angels in charge of you
   to protect you in all your ways.
¹²      They will carry you in their hands

so that you never hit your foot
against a rock.
13 You will step on lions and cobras.
You will trample young lions and snakes.

14 Because you love me, I will rescue you.
I will protect you because you know my name.
15 When you call to me, I will answer you.
I will be with you when you are in trouble.
I will save you and honor you.
16 I will satisfy you with a long life.
I will show you how I will save you.

## PROVERBS 19:1-12

1 Better to be a poor person who lives innocently
than to be one who talks dishonestly and is a fool.
2 A person without knowledge is no good.
A person in a hurry makes mistakes.
3 The stupidity of a person turns his life upside down,
and his heart rages against the LORD.
4 Wealth adds many friends,
but a poor person is separated from his friend.

5 A lying witness will not go unpunished.
One who tells lies will not escape.
6 Many try to win the kindness
of a generous person,
and everyone is a friend to a person
who gives gifts.
7 The entire family of a poor person hates him.
How much more do his friends
keep their distance from him!

> When he chases them with words,
> > they are gone.

8   A person who gains sense loves himself.
> One who guards understanding
> > finds something good.

9   A lying witness will not go unpunished.
> One who tells lies will die.

10   Luxury does not fit a fool,
> > much less a slave ruling princes.

11   A person with good sense is patient,
> and it is to his credit that he overlooks an offense.

12   The rage of a king is like the roar of a lion,
> but his favor is like dew on the grass.

# *Day 54* ≈

## PSALM 92

A psalm; a song; for the day of worship.

1   It is good to give thanks to the LORD,
> to make music to praise your name, O Most High.

2   It is good to announce your mercy in the morning
> and your faithfulness in the evening

3     on a ten-stringed instrument and a harp
> and with a melody on a lyre.

4   You made me find joy in what you have done,
> O LORD.

I will sing joyfully about the works of your hands.

5     How spectacular are your works, O LORD!
> How very deep are your thoughts!

6   A stupid person cannot know
     and a fool cannot understand
7       that wicked people sprout like grass
        and all troublemakers blossom ⌊like flowers⌋,
        only to be destroyed forever.

8   But you, O LORD, are highly honored forever.
9      Now look at your enemies, O LORD.
     Now look at your enemies.
       They disappear, and all troublemakers
       are scattered.

10   But you make me as strong as a wild bull,
     and soothing lotion is poured on me.
11   My eyes gloat over those who spy on me.
     My ears hear ⌊the cries⌋ of evildoers attacking me.

12   Righteous people flourish like palm trees
     and grow tall like the cedars in Lebanon.
13      They are planted in the LORD's house.
       They blossom in our God's courtyards.
14       Even when they are old, they still bear fruit.
       They are always healthy and fresh.
15        They make it known that the LORD is decent.
        He is my rock.
        He is never unfair.

## PSALM 93

1   The LORD rules as king! He is clothed with majesty.
     The LORD has clothed himself; he has armed himself
     with power.
     The world was set in place; it cannot be moved.

2   Your throne was set in place a long time ago.
     You are eternal.

3 The ocean rises, O LORD.
The ocean rises with a roar.
The ocean rises with its pounding waves.
4 The LORD above is mighty—
mightier than the sound of raging water,
mightier than the foaming waves of the sea.

5 Your written testimonies are completely reliable.
O LORD, holiness is what makes your house beautiful
for days without end.

## PROVERBS 19:13-22

### A Foolish Son Brings Ruin to Others

13 A foolish son ruins his father,
and a quarreling woman is like
constantly dripping water.
14 Home and wealth are inherited from fathers,
but a sensible wife comes from the LORD.

15 Laziness throws one into a deep sleep,
and an idle person will go hungry.
16 Whoever obeys the law preserves his life,
⌊but⌋ whoever despises the LORD's ways
will be put to death.

17 Whoever has pity on the poor lends to the LORD,
and he will repay him for his good deed.
18 Discipline your son while there is still hope.
Do not be the one responsible for his death.
19 A person who has a hot temper will pay for it.
If you rescue him,
you will have to do it over and over.
20 Listen to advice and accept discipline

so that you may be wise the rest of your life.

21 Many plans are in the human heart,
but the advice of the LORD will endure.

22 Loyalty is desirable in a person,
and it is better to be poor than a liar.


# *Day 55* ⟆

## PSALM 94

1 O LORD, God of vengeance,
O God of vengeance, appear!

2 Arise, O Judge of the earth.
Give arrogant people what they deserve.

3 How long, O LORD, will wicked people triumph?
How long?

4 They ramble.
They speak arrogantly.
All troublemakers brag about themselves.

5 They crush your people, O LORD.
They make those who belong to you suffer.

6 They kill widows and foreigners,
and they murder orphans.

7 They say, "The LORD doesn't see it.
The God of Jacob
doesn't even pay attention to it."

8 Pay attention, you stupid people!
When will you become wise, you fools?

9 God created ears.
Do you think he can't hear?
He formed eyes.

Do you think he can't see?
10 He disciplines nations.
Do you think he can't punish?
He teaches people.
Do you think he doesn't know anything?
11 The LORD knows that people's thoughts
are pointless.

12 O LORD, blessed is the person
whom you discipline and instruct
from your teachings.
13 You give him peace and quiet from times
of trouble
while a pit is dug to trap wicked people.

14 The LORD will never desert his people
or abandon those who belong to him.
15 The decisions of judges will again become fair,
and everyone whose motives are decent
will pursue justice.[a]

16 Who will stand up for me against evildoers?
Who will stand by my side against troublemakers?
17 If the LORD had not come to help me,
my soul would have quickly fallen silent
⸤in death⸥.

18 When I said, "My feet are slipping,"
your mercy, O LORD, continued to hold me up.
19 When I worried about many things,
your assuring words soothed my soul.

20 Are wicked rulers who use the law
to do unlawful things

---

[a] 94:15 English equivalent of this verse difficult.

able to be your partners?
21     They join forces to take the lives
           of righteous people.
       They condemn innocent people to death.
22 The LORD has become my stronghold.
   My God has become my rock of refuge.
23     He has turned their own wickedness against them.
       He will destroy them because of their sins.
       The LORD our God will destroy them.

### PROVERBS 19:23-29

23 The fear of the LORD leads to life,
       and such a person will rest easy
           without suffering harm.[a]
24 A lazy person puts his fork in his food.
       He doesn't even bring it back to his mouth.
25 Strike a mocker,
           and a gullible person may learn a lesson.
       Warn an understanding person,
           and he will gain more knowledge.

### Foolproof Instructions

26     A son who assaults his father
           ‚and‚ who drives away his mother
       brings shame and disgrace.
27 If you stop listening to instruction, my son,
       you will stray from the words of knowledge.

28 A worthless witness mocks justice,
       and the mouths of wicked people
           swallow up trouble.

---

[a] 19:23 Hebrew meaning of this line uncertain.

29　　Punishments are set for mockers
　　　　　and beatings for the backs of fools.


# *Day 56* ⁂

## PSALM 95

1　Come, let's sing joyfully to the LORD.
　　　Let's shout happily to the rock of our salvation.
2　　　Let's come into his presence with a song
　　　　　of thanksgiving.
　　　Let's shout happily to him with psalms.
3　The LORD is a great God and a great king
　　　　above all gods.
4　　In his hand are the deep places of the earth,
　　　　and the mountain peaks are his.
5　　The sea is his.
　　　He made it, and his hands formed the dry land.

6　Come, let's worship and bow down.
　　　Let's kneel in front of the LORD, our maker,
7　　　because he is our God
　　　　　and we are the people in his care,
　　　　　　the flock that he leads.
　　If only you would listen to him today!
8　　"Do not be stubborn like my people
　　　　were at Meribah,
　　　　like the time at Massah in the desert.
9　　　Your ancestors challenged me
　　　　　and tested me there,
　　　　　　although they had seen what I had done.
10　For 40 years I was disgusted with those people.

So I said, 'They are a people whose hearts
      continue to stray.
   They have not learned my ways.'
11   That is why I angrily took this solemn oath:
      'They will never enter my place of rest!' "

## PSALM 96

1  Sing to the LORD a new song!
    Sing to the LORD, all the earth!
2  Sing to the LORD! Praise his name!
     Day after day announce that the LORD
       saves his people.
3     Tell people about his glory.
     Tell all the nations about his miracles.

4  The LORD is great!
    He should be highly praised.
    He should be feared more than all ˻other˼ gods
5     because all the gods of the nations are idols.
  The LORD made the heavens.
6    Splendor and majesty are in his presence.
    Strength and beauty are in his holy place.

7  Give to the LORD, you families of the nations.
    Give to the LORD glory and power.
8  Give to the LORD the glory he deserves.
    Bring an offering, and come into his courtyards.
9    Worship the LORD in ˻his˼ holy splendor.
    Tremble in his presence, all the earth!

10  Say to the nations, "The LORD rules as king!"
    The earth stands firm; it cannot be moved.
    He will judge people fairly.
11    Let the heavens rejoice and the earth be glad.

Let the sea and everything in it roar like thunder.
12 Let the fields and everything in them rejoice.
   Then all the trees in the forest will sing joyfully
13 in the LORD's presence
      because he is coming.
   He is coming to judge the earth.
   He will judge the world
      with righteousness
      and its people with his truth.

## PROVERBS 20:1-8

1 Wine ˏmakes people˲ mock,
   liquor ˏmakes them˲ noisy,
      and everyone under their influence is unwise.
2 The rage of a king is like the roar of a lion.
   Whoever makes him angry forfeits his life.
3 Avoiding a quarrel is honorable.
   After all, any stubborn fool can start a fight.

4 A lazy person does not plow in the fall.[a]
   He looks for something in the harvest
      but finds nothing.
5 A motive in the human heart is like deep water,
   and a person who has understanding draws it out.
6 Many people declare themselves loyal,
   but who can find someone
      who is ˏreally˲ trustworthy?
7 A righteous person lives on the basis of his integrity.
   Blessed are his children after he is gone.
8 A king who sits on his throne to judge
   sifts out every evil with his eyes.

---

[a] 20:4 Fall was the start of the planting season in Palestine.

# *Day 57* ≈

## PSALM 97

1 The LORD rules as king.
   Let the earth rejoice.
   Let all the islands be joyful.
2 Clouds and darkness surround him.
   Righteousness and justice are the foundations
        of his throne.
3 Fire spreads ahead of him.
   It burns his enemies who surround him.
4 His flashes of lightning light up the world.
        The earth sees them and trembles.
5 The mountains melt like wax in the presence
        of the LORD,
   in the presence of the Lord of the whole earth.
6 The heavens tell about his righteousness,
        and all the people of the world see his glory.

7 Everyone who worships idols
        and brags about false gods will be put to shame.
   All the gods will bow to him.

8 Zion hears about this and rejoices.
   The people of Judah are delighted
        with your judgments, O LORD.
9 You, O LORD, the Most High,
        are above the whole earth.
   You are highest. You are above all the gods.
10 Let those who love the LORD hate evil.
   The one who guards the lives of his godly ones

will rescue them from the power of wicked people.
11 Light dawns for righteous people[a]
and joy for those whose motives are decent.
12 Find joy in the LORD, you righteous people.
Give thanks to him as you remember how holy he is.

## PSALM 98

A psalm.

1 Sing a new song to the LORD
because he has done miraculous things.
His right hand and his holy arm
have gained victory for him.
2 The LORD has made his salvation known.
He has uncovered his righteousness
for the nations to see.
3 He has not forgotten to be merciful and faithful
to Israel's descendants.
All the ends of the earth have seen
how our God saves ˻them˼.

4 Shout happily to the LORD, all the earth.
Break out into joyful singing, and make music.
5 Make music to the LORD with a lyre,
with a lyre and the melody of a psalm,
6 with trumpets and the playing of a ram's horn.
Shout happily in the presence of the king, the LORD.

7 Let the sea, everything in it,
the world, and those who live in it roar
like thunder.

---

[a] 97:11 One Hebrew manuscript, Greek, Syriac, Latin; other Hebrew manuscripts "Light is planted for righteous people."

8    Let the rivers clap their hands
         and the mountains sing joyfully
9          in the LORD's presence
               because he is coming to judge the earth.
               He will judge the world with justice
                 and its people with fairness.


### PROVERBS 20:9-19

9    Who can say,
         "I've made my heart pure.
         I'm cleansed from my sin"?
10   A double standard of weights and measures—
         both are disgusting to the LORD.
11   Even a child makes himself known by his actions,
         whether his deeds are pure or right.
12   The ear that hears,
         the eye that sees—
             the LORD made them both.
13   Do not love sleep or you will end up poor.
     Keep your eyes open,
         and you will have plenty to eat.

14   "Bad! Bad!" says the buyer.
         Then, as he goes away,
             he brags ˌabout his bargainˌ.
15   There are gold and plenty of jewels,
         but the lips of knowledge are precious gems.
16   Hold on to the garment of one who guarantees
             a stranger's loan,
         and hold responsible the person
             who makes a loan on behalf of a foreigner.

<sup>17</sup> Food gained dishonestly tastes sweet to a person,
  but afterwards his mouth will be filled with gravel.

<sup>18</sup> Plans are confirmed by getting advice,
  and with guidance one wages war.

<sup>19</sup> Whoever goes around as a gossip tells secrets.
  Do not associate with a person whose mouth
   is always open.

# *Day 58* &#x2767;

## PSALM 99

<sup>1</sup> The LORD rules as king.
  Let the people tremble.
He is enthroned over the angels.[a]
  Let the earth quake.

<sup>2</sup> The LORD is mighty in Zion.
He is high above all people.

<sup>3</sup>   Let them give thanks to your great
   and fearful name.

  He is holy!

<sup>4</sup> The king's strength is that he loves justice.
  You have established fairness.
  You have done what is fair and right for Jacob.

<sup>5</sup> Highly honor the LORD our God.
  Bow down at his footstool.

  He is holy!

---

[a] 99:1 Or "cherubim."

⁶ Moses and Aaron were among his priests.
Samuel was among those who prayed to him.
   They called to the LORD, and he answered them.
⁷     He spoke to them from a column of smoke.
They obeyed his written instructions and the laws
    that he gave them.
⁸ O LORD, our God, you answered them.
   ` You showed them that you are a forgiving God
    and that you are a God
      who punishes their ˌsinfulˌ deeds.

⁹ Highly honor the LORD our God.
Bow at his holy mountain.

   The LORD our God is holy!

## PSALM 100

A psalm of thanksgiving.

¹ Shout happily to the LORD, all the earth.
² Serve the LORD cheerfully.
Come into his presence with a joyful song.
³ Realize that the LORD alone is God.
   He made us, and we are his.ᵃ
   We are his people and the sheep in his care.
⁴ Enter his gates with a song of thanksgiving.
Come into his courtyards with a song of praise.
Give thanks to him; praise his name.

⁵ The LORD is good.
   His mercy endures forever.

---

ᵃ 100:3 Many Hebrew manuscripts, Greek, Targum, Latin; other Hebrew manuscripts "and not
we ourselves."

His faithfulness endures
throughout every generation.


## PSALM 101

A psalm by David.

1　I will sing about mercy and justice.
O LORD, I will make music to praise you.
2　I want to understand the path to integrity.
When will you come to me?

I will live in my own home with integrity.
3　I will not put anything wicked in front of my eyes.
I hate what unfaithful people do.
I want no part of it.
4　I will keep far away from devious minds.
I will have nothing to do with evil.
5　I will destroy anyone who secretly
slanders his neighbor.
I will not tolerate anyone with a conceited look
or arrogant heart.
6　My eyes will be watching the faithful people in the land
so that they may live with me.
The person who lives with integrity will serve me.

7　The one who does deceitful things will not stay
in my home.
The one who tells lies will not remain
in my presence.

8　Every morning I will destroy all the wicked people
in the land
to rid the LORD's city of all troublemakers.

## PROVERBS 20:20-30

20   The lamp of the person who curses his father
           and mother
         will be snuffed out in total darkness.[a]
21   An inheritance quickly obtained in the beginning
         will never be blessed in the end.
22   Do not say, "I'll get even with you!"
         Wait for the LORD, and he will save you.
23   A double standard of weights is disgusting
             to the LORD,
         and dishonest scales are no good.
24   The LORD is the one who directs a person's steps.
         How then can anyone understand his own way?
25   It is a trap for a person to say impulsively,
             "This is a holy offering!"
         and later to have second thoughts
             about those vows.

26   A wise king scatters the wicked
         and then runs them over.
27   A person's soul is the LORD's lamp.
         It searches his entire innermost being.
28   Mercy and truth protect a king,
         and with mercy he maintains his throne.
29   While the glory of young men is their strength,
         the splendor of older people is their silver hair.
30   Brutal beatings cleanse away wickedness.
       Such beatings cleanse the innermost being.

---

[a] 20:20 Or "snuffed out as darkness approaches."

# *Day 59* ❧

## PSALM 102

A prayer by someone who is suffering, when he is weary and pours out his troubles in the LORD's presence.

¹ O LORD, hear my prayer,
and let my cry for help come to you.
² Do not hide your face from me
when I am in trouble.
Turn your ear toward me.
Answer me quickly when I call.
³ My days disappear like smoke.
My bones burn like hot coals.
⁴ My heart is beaten down and withered like grass
because I have forgotten about eating.
⁵ I am nothing but skin and bones
because of my loud groans.
⁶ I am like a desert owl,
like an owl living in the ruins.
⁷ I lie awake.
I am like a lonely bird on a rooftop.
⁸ All day long my enemies insult me.
Those who ridicule me use my name as a curse.
⁹ I eat ashes like bread
and my tears are mixed with my drink
¹⁰ because of your hostility and anger,
because you have picked me up
and thrown me away.
¹¹ My days are like a shadow that is getting longer,
and I wither away like grass.

12   But you, O LORD, remain forever.
         You are remembered
             throughout every generation.
13   You will rise and have compassion on Zion,
         because it is time to grant a favor to it.
             Indeed, the appointed time has come.
14             Your servants value Zion's stones,
                 and they pity its rubble.
15   The nations will fear the LORD's name.
     All the kings of the earth will fear your glory.
16   When the LORD builds Zion,
         he will appear in his glory.
17   He will turn his attention to the prayers
         of those who have been abandoned.
     He will not despise their prayers.
18   This will be written down for a future generation
         so that a people yet to be created
             may praise the LORD:
19         "The LORD looked down from his holy place
                 high above.
         From heaven he looked at the earth.
20             He heard the groans of the prisoners
                 and set free those who were condemned
                     to death.
21                 The LORD's name is announced in Zion
                     and his praise in Jerusalem
22                     when nations and kingdoms gather
                         to worship the LORD."

23   He has weakened my strength along the way.
     He has reduced ˌthe number ofˌ my days.
24   I said, "My God, don't take me now in the middle
         of my life.

Your years ⸤continue on⸥
    throughout every generation.
<sup>25</sup> Long ago you laid the foundation of the earth.
    Even the heavens are the works of your hands.
<sup>26</sup> They will come to an end, but you will still go on.
    They will all wear out like clothing.
      You will change them like clothes,
        and they will be thrown away.
<sup>27</sup>       But you remain the same,
          and your life will never end.
<sup>28</sup> The children of your servants
    will go on living ⸤here⸥.
Their descendants will be secure
    in your presence."

## PROVERBS 21:1-12

### The LORD Controls Wise and Foolish People

<sup>1</sup> The king's heart is like streams of water.
    Both are under the LORD's control.
      He turns them in any direction he chooses.
<sup>2</sup> A person thinks everything he does is right,
    but the LORD weighs hearts.
<sup>3</sup> Doing what is right and fair
    is more acceptable to the LORD
      than offering a sacrifice.
<sup>4</sup> A conceited look and an arrogant attitude,
    which are the lamps of wicked people, are sins.

<sup>5</sup> The plans of a hard-working person lead
    to prosperity,
    but everyone who is ⸤always⸥ in a hurry
      ends up in poverty.

⁶ Those who gather wealth by lying are wasting time.
    They are looking for death.
⁷ The violence of wicked people will drag them away
    since they refuse to do what is just.
⁸ The way of a guilty person is crooked,
    but the behavior of those who are pure is moral.ᵃ

⁹ Better to live on a corner of a roof
    than to share a home with a quarreling woman.
¹⁰ The mind of a wicked person desires evil
    and has no consideration for his neighbor.
¹¹ When a mocker is punished,
     a gullible person becomes wise,
    and when a wise person is instructed,
     he gains knowledge.
¹² A righteous person wisely considers the house
    of a wicked person.
    He throws wicked people into disasters.

# *Day 60* ≋

## PSALM 103

By David.

¹ Praise the LORD, my soul!
    Praise his holy name, all that is within me.
² Praise the LORD, my soul,
     and never forget all the good he has done:
³     He is the one who forgives all your sins,
     the one who heals all your diseases,
⁴      the one who rescues your life from the pit,

---

ᵃ 21:8 Hebrew meaning of this verse uncertain.

the one who crowns you
with mercy and compassion,
⁵ the one who fills your life with blessings
so that you become young again
like an eagle.

⁶ The LORD does what is right and fair
for all who are oppressed.
⁷ He let Moses know his ways.
He let the Israelites know the things
he had done.
⁸ The LORD is compassionate, merciful, patient,
and always ready to forgive.

⁹ He will not always accuse us of wrong
or be angry ⸢with us⸥ forever.
¹⁰ He has not treated us as we deserve for our sins
or paid us back for our wrongs.

¹¹ As high as the heavens are above the earth—
that is how vast his mercy is toward those
who fear him.
¹² As far as the east is from the west—
that is how far he has removed our rebellious acts
from himself.
¹³ As a father has compassion for his children,
so the LORD has compassion for those who fear him.

¹⁴ He certainly knows what we are made of.
He bears in mind that we are dust.
¹⁵ Human life is as short-lived as grass.
It blossoms like a flower in the field.
¹⁶ When the wind blows over the flower,
it disappears,
and there is no longer any sign of it.

17 But from everlasting to everlasting,
    the LORD's mercy is on those who fear him.
      His righteousness belongs
        to their children and grandchildren,
18         to those who are faithful to his promise,*a*
      to those who remember to follow
        his guiding principles.
19 The LORD has set his throne in heaven.
    His kingdom rules everything.

20 Praise the LORD, all his angels,
    you mighty beings who carry out his orders
      and are ready to obey his spoken orders.
21 Praise the LORD, all his armies,
    his servants who carry out his will.
22 Praise the LORD, all his creatures
    in all the places of his empire.
    Praise the LORD, my soul!

## PROVERBS 21:13-21

13 Whoever shuts his ear to the cry of the poor
    will call and not be answered.
14 A gift ⌊given⌋ in secret calms anger,
    and a secret bribe calms great fury.
15 When justice is done,
    a righteous person is delighted,
    but troublemakers are terrified.
16 A person who wanders from the way
    of wise behavior
    will rest in the assembly of the dead.

---

*a* 103:18 Or "covenant."

17  Whoever loves pleasure will become poor.
    Whoever loves wine and expensive food
        will not become rich.
18      Wicked people become a ransom
            for righteous people,
                and treacherous people will take the place
                    of decent people.
19  Better to live in a desert
        than with a quarreling and angry woman.
20  Costly treasure and wealth are in the home
        of a wise person,
        but a fool devours them.
21  Whoever pursues righteousness and mercy
        will find life, righteousness, and honor.

# *Day 61* &#8766;

## PSALM 104

1  Praise the LORD, my soul!
    O LORD my God, you are very great.
        You are clothed with splendor and majesty.
2      You cover yourself with light
            as though it were a robe.
        You stretch out the heavens
            as though they were curtains.
3      You lay the beams of your home in the water.
        You use the clouds for your chariot.
        You move on the wings of the wind.
4      You make your angels winds
            and your servants flames of fire.

5   You set the earth on its foundations
        so that it can never be shaken.
6   You covered the earth with an ocean
        as though it were a robe.
    Water stood above the mountains
7       and fled because of your threat.
    Water ran away at the sound of your thunder.
8       The mountains rose and the valleys sank
            to the place you appointed for them.
9   Water cannot cross the boundary you set
        and cannot come back to cover the earth.

10  You make water gush from springs into valleys.
        It flows between the mountains.
11      Every wild animal drinks ˌfrom themˌ.
        Wild donkeys quench their thirst.
12          The birds live by the streams.
            They sing among the branches.
13  You water the mountains from your home above.
    You fill the earth with the fruits of your labors.

14  You make grass grow for cattle
        and make vegetables for humans to use
            in order to get food from the ground.
15  You make wine to cheer human hearts,
        olive oil to make faces shine,
            and bread to strengthen human hearts.
16  The LORD's trees, the cedars in Lebanon
        which he planted,
        drink their fill.
17      Birds build their nests in them.
        Storks makes their homes in fir trees.
18  The high mountains are for wild goats.
    The rocks are a refuge for badgers.

<sup>19</sup> He created the moon, which marks the seasons,
and the sun, which knows when to set.

<sup>20</sup> He brings darkness, and it is nighttime,
when all the wild animals in the forest
come out.

<sup>21</sup> The young lions roar for their prey
and seek their food from God.

<sup>22</sup> When the sun rises,
they gather and lie down in their dens.

<sup>23</sup> Then people go to do their work,
to do their tasks until evening.

<sup>24</sup> What a large number of things you have made,
O Lord!
You made them all by wisdom.
The earth is filled with your creatures.

<sup>25</sup> The sea is so big and wide
with countless creatures,
living things both large and small.

<sup>26</sup> Ships sail on it,
and Leviathan,<sup>a</sup> which you made,
plays in it.

<sup>27</sup> All of them look to you to give them their food
at the right time.

<sup>28</sup> You give it to them, and they gather it up.
You open your hand,
and they are filled with blessings.

<sup>29</sup> You hide your face, and they are terrified.
You take away their breath, and they die
and return to dust.

<sup>30</sup> You send out your Spirit, and they are created.
You renew the face of the earth.

---

[a] 104:26 Hebrew meaning uncertain.

31 May the glory of the LORD endure forever.
May the LORD find joy in what he has made.

32 He looks at the earth, and it trembles.
He touches the mountains, and they smoke.

33 I will sing to the LORD throughout my life.
I will make music to praise my God
as long as I live.

34 May my thoughts be pleasing to him.
I will find joy in the LORD.

35 May sinners vanish from the world.
May there no longer be any wicked people.
Praise the LORD, my soul!

Hallelujah!


## PROVERBS 21:22-31

22 A wise man attacks a city of warriors
and pulls down the strong defenses
in which they trust.

23 Whoever guards his mouth and his tongue
keeps himself out of trouble.

24 An arrogant, conceited person is called a mocker.
His arrogance knows no limits.

25 The desire of a lazy person will kill him
because his hands refuse to work.

26 All day long he feels greedy,
but a righteous person gives
and does not hold back.

27 The sacrifice of wicked people is disgusting,
especially if they bring it with evil intent.

28 A lying witness will die,

but a person who listens to advice
    will continue to speak.
29 A wicked person puts up a bold front,
    but a decent person's way of life
        is his own security.

30 No wisdom, no understanding, and no advice
    ˌcan stand upˌ against the LORD.
31 The horse is made ready for the day of battle,
    but the victory belongs to the LORD.

# *Day 62* ❧

## PSALM 105

1 Give thanks to the LORD.
  Call on him.
  Make known among the nations what he has done.
2 Sing to him.
  Make music to praise him.
  Meditate on all the miracles he has performed.
3 Brag about his holy name.
  Let the hearts of those who seek the LORD rejoice.
4 Search for the LORD and his strength.
  Always seek his presence.
5 Remember the miracles he performed,
    the amazing things he did, and the judgments
      he pronounced,
6     you descendants of his servant Abraham,
    you descendants of Jacob, his chosen ones.

7  He is the LORD our God.
    His judgments are pronounced
        throughout the earth.
8  He always remembers his promise,[a]
    the word that he commanded
        for a thousand generations,
9      the promise that he made to Abraham,
        and his sworn oath to Isaac.
10  He confirmed it as a law for Jacob,
    as an everlasting promise to Israel,
11      by saying, "I will give you the land of Canaan.
        It is your share of the inheritance."

12  While the people of Israel were few in number,
    a small group of foreigners living in that land,
13      they wandered from nation to nation,
        from one kingdom to another.
14  He didn't permit anyone to oppress them.
    He warned kings about them:
15      "Do not touch my anointed ones
        or harm my prophets."

16  He brought famine to the land.
    He took away their food supply.
17  He sent a man ahead of them.
    He sent Joseph, who was sold as a slave.
18      They hurt his feet with shackles,
        and cut into his neck with an iron collar.
19          The LORD's promise tested him
            through fiery trials
            until his prediction came true.
20      The king sent someone to release him.
    The ruler of nations set him free.

---

[a] 105:8 Or "covenant."

21     He made Joseph the master of his palace
        and the ruler of all his possessions.
22         Joseph trained the king's officers
           the way he wanted
                and taught his respected leaders wisdom.

23     Then Israel came to Egypt.
        Jacob lived as a foreigner in the land of Ham.
24     The Lord made his people grow rapidly in number
        and stronger than their enemies.
25     He changed their minds so that they hated
        his people,
        and they dealt treacherously with his servants.
26     He sent his servant Moses, and he sent Aaron,
        whom he had chosen.
27         They displayed his miraculous signs among them
           and did amazing things in the land of Ham.
28     He sent darkness and made ˌtheir landˌ dark.
        They did not rebel against his orders.
29     He turned their water into blood
        and caused their fish to die.
30     He made their land swarm with frogs,
        even in the kings' bedrooms.
31     He spoke, and swarms of flies and gnats
        infested their whole territory.
32     He gave them hail and lightning
        instead of rain throughout their land.
33     He struck their grapevines and fig trees
        and smashed the trees in their territory.
34     He spoke,
           and countless locusts and grasshoppers came.
35         They devoured all the plants in the land.
        They devoured the crops in the fields.

36 He killed all the firstborn sons,
     the first ones born in the land
          when their fathers were young.

37 He brought Israel out with silver and gold,
     and no one among his tribes stumbled.

38 The Egyptians were terrified of Israel,
     so they were glad when Israel left.

39 He spread out a cloud as a protective covering
     and a fire to light up the night.

40 The Israelites asked, and he brought them quail
     and filled them with bread from heaven.

41 He opened a rock, and water gushed
     and flowed like a river through the dry places.

42 He remembered his holy promise
     to his servant Abraham.

43 He brought his people out with joy,
     his chosen ones with a song of joy.

44 He gave them the lands of ⌊other⌋ nations,
     and they inherited what others had worked for

45      so that they would obey his laws
          and follow his teachings.

Hallelujah!

## PROVERBS 22:1-12

1 A good name is more desirable than great wealth.
     Respect is better than silver or gold.

2 The rich and the poor have this in common:
     the LORD is the maker of them all.

3 Sensible people foresee trouble and hide ⌊from it⌋,
     but gullible people go ahead
          and suffer ⌊the consequence⌋.

⁴  On the heels of humility (the fear of the LORD)
      are riches and honor and life.

⁵  A devious person has thorns and traps
         ahead of him.
      Whoever guards himself will stay far away
         from them.

⁶  Train a child in the way he should go,
      and even when he is old he will not turn away
         from it.

⁷  A rich person rules poor people,
      and a borrower is a slave to a lender.

⁸  Whoever plants injustice will harvest trouble,
      and this weapon of his own fury will be destroyed.

⁹  Whoever is generous will be blessed
      because he has shared his food with the poor.

¹⁰ Drive out a mocker, and conflict will leave.
      Quarreling and abuse will stop.

¹¹ Whoever loves a pure heart
      and whoever speaks graciously
         has a king as his friend.

¹² The LORD's eyes watch over knowledge,
      but he overturns the words
         of a treacherous person.

# *Day 63* ✺

## PSALM 106

¹  Hallelujah!

Give thanks to the LORD because he is good,
      because his mercy endures forever.

² Who can speak about all the mighty things
     the LORD has done?
Who can announce all the things for which
     he is worthy of praise?
³ Blessed are those who defend justice
     and do what is right at all times.

⁴ Remember me, O LORD, when you show favor
     to your people.
Come to help me with your salvation
⁵      so that I may see the prosperity
        of your chosen ones,
        find joy in our people's happiness,
           and brag with the people who belong to you.

⁶ We have sinned, and so did our ancestors.
We have done wrong.
We are guilty.
⁷      When our ancestors were in Egypt,
        they gave no thought to your miracles.
           They did not remember your numerous acts
              of mercy,
                so they rebelled at the sea, the Red Sea.

⁸ He saved them because of his reputation
     so that he could make his mighty power known.
⁹ He angrily commanded the Red Sea, and it dried up.
He led them through deep water
     as though it were a desert.
¹⁰ He rescued them from the power of the one
     who hated them.
He rescued them from the enemy.
¹¹      Water covered their adversaries.
        Not one Egyptian survived.

12          Then our ancestors believed what he said.
                They sang his praise.

13     They quickly forgot what he did.
          They did not wait for his advice.
14     They had an unreasonable desire ˌfor foodˌ
                in the wilderness.
          In the desert they tested God.
15          He gave them what they asked for.
          He ˌalsoˌ gave them a degenerative disease.

16     In the camp certain men became envious of Moses.
          They also became envious of Aaron,
                the LORD's holy one.
17          The ground split open and swallowed Dathan.
                It buried Abiram's followers.
18               A fire broke out among their followers.
                Flames burned up wicked people.

19     At Mount Horeb they made ˌa statue ofˌ a calf.
          They worshiped an idol made of metal.
20          They traded their glorious God*a*
                for the statue of a bull that eats grass.
21     They forgot God, their savior,
          the one who did spectacular things in Egypt,
22          miracles in the land of Ham,
                and terrifying things at the Red Sea.
23     God said he was going to destroy them,
          but Moses, his chosen one, stood in his way
                to prevent him from exterminating them.

24     They refused ˌto enterˌ the pleasant land.
          They did not believe what he said.

---

*a* 106:20 Or "their glory."

25 They complained in their tents.
They did not obey the LORD.
26     Raising his hand, he swore
       that he would kill them in the wilderness,
27          kill their descendants among the nations,
      and scatter them
         throughout various lands.

28 They joined in worshiping the god Baal
    while they were at Peor,
  and they ate what was sacrificed to the dead.
29 They infuriated God by what they did,
  and a plague broke out among them.
30 Then Phinehas stood between God and the people,
  and the plague was stopped.
31     Because of this, Phinehas was considered
      righteous forever,
       throughout every generation.
32 They made God angry by the water at Meribah.
  Things turned out badly for Moses
    because of what they did,
33     since they made him bitter
      so that he spoke recklessly.

34 They did not destroy the people
  as the LORD had told them.
35     Instead, they intermarried with other nations.
    They learned to do what other nations did,
36       and they worshiped their idols,
       which became a trap for them.
37 They sacrificed their sons and daughters to demons.
38     They shed innocent blood,
      the blood of their own sons and daughters
       whom they sacrificed to the idols of Canaan.

The land became polluted with blood.
39 They became filthy because of what they did.
They behaved like prostitutes.
40        The LORD burned with anger
                against his own people.
         He was disgusted with those who belonged
                to him.
41        He handed them over to other nations,
                and those who hated them ruled them.
42                Their enemies oppressed them
                        and made them subject to their power.
43        He rescued them many times,
                but they continued to plot rebellion
                        against him
                and to sink deeper because of their sin.
44        He saw that they were suffering
                when he heard their cry for help.
45        He remembered his promise*a* to them.
                In keeping with his rich mercy,
                        he changed his plans.
46        He let them find compassion
                from all those who held them captive.

47   Rescue us, O LORD our God, and gather us
                from the nations
         so that we may give thanks to your holy name
                and make your praise our glory.

48                Thanks be to the LORD God of Israel
                        from everlasting to everlasting.
                        Let all the people say amen.

                        Hallelujah!

---

*a* 106:45 Or "covenant."

## PROVERBS 22:13-21

13  A lazy person says,
        "There's a lion outside!
            I'll be murdered in the streets!"
14  The mouth of an adulterous woman is a deep pit.
        The one who is cursed by the LORD will fall into it.
15  Foolishness is firmly attached to a child's heart.
        Spanking will remove it far from him.
16  Oppressing the poor for profit
        ˌorˌ giving to the rich
            certainly leads to poverty.

### Listen to My Advice

17  Open your ears, and hear the words of wise people,
        and set your mind on the knowledge I give you.
18          It is pleasant if you keep them in mind
                ˌso thatˌ they will be on the tip of your tongue,
19          so that your trust may be in the LORD.
        Today I have made them known to you,
            especially to you.
20  Didn't I write to you previously with advice
        and knowledge
21  in order to teach you the words of truth
        so that you can give an accurate report
            to those who send you?

# *Day 64* ✎

## PSALM 107

1   Give thanks to the LORD because he is good,
        because his mercy endures forever.

2    Let the people the LORD defended
      repeat these words.
        They are the people he defended from the power
           of their enemies
3       and gathered from other countries,
        from the east and from the west,
        from the north and from the south.
4    They wandered around the desert
      on a deserted road
      without finding an inhabited city.
5    They were hungry and thirsty.
   They began to lose hope.
6  In their distress they cried out to the LORD.
   He rescued them from their troubles.
7    He led them on a road that went straight
      to an inhabited city.

8   Let them give thanks to the LORD because
     of his mercy.
     He performed his miracles for Adam's descendants.
9      He gave plenty to drink to those who were thirsty.
     He filled those who were hungry with good food.
10       Those who lived in the dark, in death's shadow
        were prisoners in misery.
        They were held in iron chains
11           because they had rebelled
           against God's words
            and had despised the advice given
              by the Most High.
12       So he humbled them with hard work.
        They fell down, but no one was there
          to help them.
13  In their distress they cried out to the LORD.

He saved them from their troubles.
14 He brought them out of the dark,
    out of death's shadow.
He broke apart their chains.

15 Let them give thanks to the LORD
    because of his mercy.
He performed his miracles
    for Adam's descendants.
16 He shattered bronze gates
    and cut iron bars in two.
17 Fools suffered because of their disobedience
    and because of their crimes.
18 All food was disgusting to them,
    and they came near death's gates.
19 In their distress they cried out to the LORD.
He saved them from their troubles.
20 He sent his message and healed them.
He rescued them from the grave.

21 Let them give thanks to the LORD
    because of his mercy.
He performed his miracles
    for Adam's descendants.
22 Let them bring songs of thanksgiving
    as their sacrifice.
Let them tell in joyful songs what he has done.
23 Those who sail on the sea in ships,
    who do business on the high seas,
24     have seen what the LORD can do,
        the miracles he performed in the depths
        of the sea.
25 He spoke, and a storm began to blow,
    and it made the waves rise high.

26     The sailors aboard ship rose toward the sky.
        They plunged into the depths.
            Their courage melted in the face of disaster.
27     They reeled and staggered like drunks,
        and all their skills as sailors became useless.
28 In their distress they cried out to the LORD.
    He led them from their troubles.
29 He made the storm calm down,
    and the waves became still.
30     The sailors were glad
        that the storm was quiet.
    He guided them to the harbor
        they had longed for.

31 Let them give thanks to the LORD
    because of his mercy.
    He performed his miracles
        for Adam's descendants.
32 Let them glorify him when the people are gathered
    for worship.
    Let them praise him in the company
        of respected leaders.
33     He changes rivers into a desert,
        springs into thirsty ground,
34         and fertile ground into a layer of salt
            because of the wickedness
                of the people living there.
35     He changes deserts into lakes
        and dry ground into springs.
36         There he settles those who are hungry,
            and they build cities to live in.
37         They plant in fields and vineyards
            that produce crops.

38      He blesses them, and their numbers multiply,
            and he does not allow a shortage of cattle.

39      They became few in number and were humiliated
            because of oppression, disaster, and sorrow.
40              He poured contempt
                    on their influential people
                and made them stumble around
                    in a pathless desert.
41              But now he lifts needy people high
                    above suffering
                and makes their families like flocks.
42                  Decent people will see this and rejoice,
                        but all the wicked people
                            will shut their mouths.

43      Let those who ⌞think⌟ they are wise
            pay attention to these things
                so that they may understand
                    the LORD's blessings.


### PROVERBS 22:22-29

*Living With Your Neighbor*

22      Do not rob the poor because they are poor
            or trample on the rights of an oppressed person
                at the city gate,
23              because the LORD will plead their case
                    and will take the lives of those
                        who rob them.
24      Do not be a friend of one who has a bad temper,
            and never keep company with a hothead,
25                  or you will learn his ways
                        and set a trap for yourself.

26　Do not be ˌfoundˌ among those who make deals
　　　　with a handshake,
　　　among those who guarantee
　　　　　other people's loans.

27　　　If you have no money to pay back a loan,
　　　　why should your bed be repossessed?

28　Do not move an ancient boundary marker
　　　that your ancestors set in place.

29　Do you see a person who is efficient in his work?
　　　He will serve kings.
　　　He will not serve unknown people.

# *Day 65* ≈

## PSALM 108[a]

A song; a psalm by David.

1　My heart is confident, O God.
　　I want to sing and make music even with my soul.[b]

2　　Wake up, harp and lyre!
　　I want to wake up at dawn.

3　I want to give thanks to you among the people,
　　　O LORD.
　　I want to make music to praise you
　　　　among the nations

4　　because your mercy is higher than the heavens.
　　　Your truth reaches the skies.

5　May you be honored above the heavens, O God.
　　Let your glory extend over the whole earth.

---

[a] 108:1 Verses 1-5 are virtually identical in wording to Psalm 57:7-11; verses 6-13 are virtually identical in wording to Psalm 60:5-12.　[b] 108:1 Or "my glory."

⁶ Save ˌusˌ with your powerful hand, and answer us
    so that those who are dear to you
        may be rescued.

⁷ God has promised the following
        through his holiness:
    "I will triumph!
        I will divide Shechem.
        I will measure the valley of Succoth.
⁸     Gilead is mine.
        Manasseh is mine.
        Ephraim is the helmet on my head.
        Judah is my scepter.
⁹     Moab is my washtub.
        I will throw my shoe over Edom.
        I will shout in triumph over Philistia."

¹⁰ Who will bring me into the fortified city?
    Who will lead me to Edom?
¹¹     Isn't it you, O God, who rejected us?
        Isn't it you, O God, who refused
            to accompany our armies?

¹² Give us help against the enemy
        because human assistance is worthless.
¹³     With God we will display great strength.
        He will trample our enemies.


## PSALM 109

For the choir director; a psalm by David.

¹ O God, whom I praise, do not turn a deaf ear to me.
² Wicked and deceitful people
        have opened their mouths against me.

They speak against me with lying tongues.

3 They surround me with hateful words.
They fight against me for no reason.

4 In return for my love, they accuse me,
but I pray for them.[a]

5 They reward me with evil instead of good
and with hatred instead of love.

6 ⌊I said,⌋ "Appoint the evil one to oppose him.
Let Satan stand beside him.

7 When he stands trial,
let him be found guilty.
Let his prayer be considered sinful.

8 Let his days be few ⌊in number⌋.
Let someone else take his position.

9 "Let his children become fatherless
and his wife a widow.

10 Let his children wander around and beg.
Let them seek help far
from their ruined homes.

11 Let a creditor take everything he owns.
Let strangers steal what he has worked for.

12 Let no one be kind to him anymore.
Let no one show any pity
to his fatherless children.

13 Let his descendants be cut off
and their family name be wiped out
by the next generation.

14 Let the LORD remember the guilt
of his ancestors
and not wipe out his mother's sin.

---

[a] 109:4 Or "but I am a man of prayer."

15             Let their guilt and sin
                always remain on record
             in front of the LORD.
            Let the LORD remove every memory of him[a]
             from the earth,

16                 because he did not remember to be kind.

            "He drove oppressed, needy,
                and brokenhearted people to their graves.

17             He loved to put curses ⌞on others⌟,
                so he, too, was cursed.
            He did not like to bless ⌞others⌟,
                so he never received a blessing.

18             He wore cursing as though it were clothing,
                so cursing entered his body like water
                and his bones like oil.

19             Let cursing be his clothing,
                a belt he always wears."

20 This is how the LORD rewards those who accuse me,
     those who say evil things against me.

21 O LORD Almighty, deal with me out of the goodness
     of your name.
     Rescue me because of your mercy.

22 I am oppressed and needy.
     I can feel the pain in my heart.

23 I fade away like a lengthening shadow.
     I have been shaken off like a grasshopper.

24      My knees give way because I have been fasting.
     My body has become lean, without any fat.

25 I have become the victim of my enemies' insults.
     They look at me and shake their heads.

---

[a] 109:15 Or "them."

26 Help me, O LORD my God.
   Save me because of your mercy.
27    Then they will know that this is your doing,
         that you, O LORD, are the one who saved me.
28 They may curse, but you will bless.
   Let those who attack me be ashamed,
      but let me rejoice.
29 Let those who accuse me wear disgrace
         as though it were clothing.
   Let them be wrapped in their shame
         as though it were a robe.

30 With my mouth I will give many thanks to the LORD.
   I will praise him among many people,
31    because he stands beside needy people
         to save them from those
            who would condemn them to death.


## PROVERBS 23:1-11

1 When you sit down to eat with a ruler,
      pay close attention to what is in front of you,
2       and put a knife to your throat
            if you have a big appetite.
3    Do not crave his delicacies,
         because this is food that deceives you.

4 Do not wear yourself out getting rich.
   Be smart enough to stop.
5    Will you catch only a fleeting glimpse of wealth
            before it is gone?
      It makes wings for itself like an eagle flying
            into the sky.

6  Do not eat the food of one who is stingy,
    and do not crave his delicacies.
7     As he calculates the cost to himself,
      this is what he does:
      He tells you, "Eat and drink,"
        but he doesn't really mean it.
8  You will vomit the little bit you have eaten
    and spoil your pleasant conversation.

9  Do not talk directly to a fool,
    because he will despise the wisdom
      of your words.
10  Do not move an ancient boundary marker
    or enter fields that belong to orphans,
11     because the one who is responsible for them
      is strong.
      He will plead their case against you.

# *Day 66* ꙳

## PSALM 110

A psalm by David.

1  The LORD said to my Lord,
    "Sit in the highest position in heaven
      until I make your enemies your footstool."

2  The LORD will extend your powerful scepter
    from Zion.
    Rule your enemies who surround you.

3     Your people will volunteer when you call
      up your army.

> Your young people will come to you
> > in holy splendor
> > like dew in the early morning.[a]

4   The LORD has taken an oath and will not change
> > his mind:
> > > "You are a priest forever, in the way Melchizedek
> > > was a priest."

5   The Lord is at your right side.
> > He will crush kings on the day of his anger.
6   He will pass judgment on the nations
> > and fill them with dead bodies.
> > > Throughout the earth
> > > > he will crush ˏtheirˎ heads.
7   He will drink from the brook along the road.
> > He will hold his head high.

## PSALM 111[b]

1   Hallelujah!

> I will give thanks to the LORD with all my heart
> > in the company of decent people
> > > and in the congregation.
2   The LORD's deeds are spectacular.
> > They should be studied by all who enjoy them.
3   His work is glorious and majestic.
> > His righteousness continues forever.
4   He has made his miracles unforgettable.
> > The LORD is merciful and compassionate.
5   He provides food for those who fear him.
> > He always remembers his promise.[c]

---

[a] 110:3 Or "You have the dew of your youth."   [b] 111:1 Psalm 111 is a poem in Hebrew alphabetical order.   [c] 111:5 Or "covenant."

6 He has revealed the power of his works
     to his people
  by giving them the lands of other nations
     as an inheritance.
7 His works are done with truth and justice.
  All his guiding principles are trustworthy.
8     They last forever and ever.
  They are carried out with truth and decency.
9 He has sent salvation to his people.
  He has ordered that his promise
    should continue forever.
  His name is holy and terrifying.
10 The fear of the LORD is the beginning of wisdom.
  Good sense is shown by everyone
    who follows ˌGod's guiding principlesˌ.
  His praise continues forever.

## PROVERBS 23:12-25

### Learning From Your Father

12 Live a more disciplined life,
  and listen carefully to words of knowledge.
13 Do not hesitate to discipline a child.
  If you spank him, he will not die.
14     Spank him yourself,
      and you will save his soul from hell.

15 My son,
  if you have a wise heart,
    my heart will rejoice as well.
16     My heart rejoices when you speak what is right.

17 Do not envy sinners in your heart.
  Instead, continue to fear the LORD.

18 There is indeed a future,
and your hope will never be cut off.

19 My son,
listen, be wise,
and keep your mind going in the right direction.

20 Do not associate with those who drink
too much wine,
with those who eat too much meat,

21 because both a drunk and a glutton
will become poor.
Drowsiness will dress a person in rags.

22 Listen to your father since you are his son,
and do not despise your mother
because she is old.

23 Buy truth (and do not sell it),
‚that is,‚ buy wisdom, discipline,
and understanding.

24 A righteous person's father will certainly rejoice.
Someone who has a wise son will enjoy him.

25 May your father and your mother be glad.
May she who gave birth to you rejoice.

# Day 67 ～

## PSALM 112[a]

1 Hallelujah!

Blessed is the person who fears the LORD
and is happy to obey his commands.

---

[a] 112:1 Psalm 112 is a poem in Hebrew alphabetical order.

2     His descendants will grow strong on the earth.
       The family of a decent person will be blessed.

3       Wealth and riches will be in his home.
       His righteousness continues forever.

4        Light will shine in the dark
         for a decent person.
          He is merciful, compassionate, and fair.

5  All goes well for the person who is generous
     and lends willingly.
  He earns an honest living.

6     He will never fail.
     A righteous person will always be remembered.

7       He is not afraid of bad news.
       His heart remains secure, full of confidence
         in the LORD.

8       His heart is steady, and he is not afraid.
        In the end he will look triumphantly
         at his enemies.

9       He gives freely to poor people.
       His righteousness continues forever.
       His head is raised in honor.

10        The wicked person sees this
         and becomes angry.
        He angrily grits his teeth and disappears.
         The hope that wicked people have
          will vanish.

## PSALM 113

1  Hallelujah!

You servants of the LORD, praise him.
Praise the name of the LORD.

2 Thank the name of the LORD now and forever.
3 From where the sun rises to where the sun sets,
    the name of the LORD should be praised.
4 The LORD is high above all the nations.
    His glory is above the heavens.
5 Who is like the LORD our God?
    He is seated on his high throne.
6 He bends down to look at heaven and earth.
7 He lifts the poor from the dust.
    He lifts the needy from a garbage heap.
8 He seats them with influential people,
    with the influential leaders of his people.
9 He makes a woman who is in a childless home
    a joyful mother.

Hallelujah!

## PROVERBS 23:26-35

26 My son,
    give me your heart.
    Let your eyes find happiness in my ways.
27     A prostitute is a deep pit.
        A loose woman is a narrow well.
28     She is like a robber, lying in ambush.
        She spreads unfaithfulness throughout society.

29 Who has trouble?
    Who has misery?
    Who has quarrels?
    Who has a complaint?
    Who has wounds for no reason?
    Who has bloodshot eyes?
30     Those who drink glass after glass of wine
        and mix it with everything.

31 Do not look at wine
because it is red,
because it sparkles in the cup,
because it goes down smoothly.
32    Later it bites like a snake
and strikes like a poisonous snake.
33 Your eyes will see strange sights,
and your mouth will say embarrassing things.
34 You will be like someone lying down
in the middle of the sea
or like someone lying down on top
of a ship's mast, saying,
35       "They strike me, but I feel no pain.
They beat me, but I'm not aware of it.
Whenever I wake up,
I'm going to look for another drink."

# Day 68 ≈

## PSALM 114

1 When Israel left Egypt,
when Jacob's family left people
who spoke a foreign language,
2    Judah became his holy place
and Israel became his kingdom.
3    The Red Sea looked at this and ran away.
The Jordan River turned back.
4       The mountains jumped like rams.
The hills jumped like lambs.
5    Red Sea, why did you run away?
Jordan River, what made you turn back?

6     Mountains, what made you jump like rams?
       Hills, what made you jump like lambs?
7  Earth, tremble in the presence of the Lord,
      in the presence of the God of Jacob.
8        He turns a rock into a pool filled with water
            and turns flint into a spring flowing with water.

## PSALM 115

1  Don't give glory to us, O LORD.
   Don't give glory to us.
      Instead, give glory to your name
         because of your mercy and faithfulness.
2  Why should other nations say, "Where is their God?"
3     Our God is in heaven.
         He does whatever he wants.
4  Their idols are made of silver and gold.
      They were made by human hands.*
5         They have mouths, but they cannot speak.
          They have eyes, but they cannot see.
6         They have ears, but they cannot hear.
          They have noses, but they cannot smell.
7         They have hands, but they cannot feel.
          They have feet, but they cannot walk.
          They cannot ˌevenˌ make a sound
             with their throats.
8            Those who make idols end up like them.
             So does everyone who trusts them.

9  Israel, trust the LORD.
      He is your helper and your shield.

---

*a* 115:4 Verses 4-8 are virtually identical in wording to Psalm 135:15-18.

10  Descendants of Aaron, trust the LORD.
       He is your helper and your shield.
11  If you fear the LORD, trust the LORD.
       He is your helper and your shield.

12  The LORD, who is ˌalwaysˌ thinking about us,
          will bless us.
       He will bless the descendants of Israel.
       He will bless the descendants of Aaron.
13     He will bless those who fear the LORD,
          from the least important to the most important.
14  May the LORD continue to bless you
          and your children.
15  You will be blessed by the LORD,
          the maker of heaven and earth.
16  The highest heaven belongs to the LORD,
          but he has given the earth to the descendants
             of Adam.
17  Those who are dead do not praise the LORD,
          nor do those who go into the silence
             ˌof the graveˌ.
18  But we will thank the LORD now and forever.

    Hallelujah!

## PROVERBS 24:1-9

1  Do not envy evil people
       or wish you were with them,
2          because their minds plot violence,
          and their lips talk trouble.

3  With wisdom a house is built.
   With understanding it is established.
4  With knowledge its rooms are filled

with every kind of riches,
both precious and pleasant.

5 A strong man knows how to use his strength,
but a person with knowledge
is even more powerful.
6 After all, with the right strategy
you can wage war,
and with many advisers there is victory.

7 Matters of wisdom are beyond the grasp
of a stubborn fool.
At the city gate he does not open his mouth.
8 Whoever plans to do evil will be known as a schemer.
9 Foolish scheming is sinful,
and a mocker is disgusting to everyone.

# *Day 69* ⁓

## PSALM 116

1 I love the LORD because he hears my voice,
my pleas for mercy.
2 I will call on him as long as I live
because he turns his ear toward me.
3 The ropes of death became tangled around me.
The horrors of the grave took hold of me.
I experienced pain and agony.

4   But I kept calling on the name of the LORD:
        "Please, LORD, rescue me!"

5   The LORD is merciful and righteous.
     Our God is compassionate.
6   The LORD protects defenseless people.
        When I was weak, he saved me.
7   Be at peace again, my soul,
        because the LORD has been good to you.

8   You saved me from death.
     You saved my eyes from tears
        ˌandˌ my feet from stumbling.
9   I will walk in the LORD's presence in this world
        of the living.
10  I kept my faith even when I said,
        "I am suffering terribly."
11  I also said when I was panic-stricken,
        "Everyone is undependable."
12  How can I repay the LORD
        for all the good that he has done for me?
13  I will take the cup of salvation
        and call on the name of the LORD.
14  I will keep my vows to the LORD
        in the presence of all his people.
15  Precious in the sight of the LORD
        is the death of his faithful ones.
16  O LORD, I am indeed your servant.
        I am your servant,
            the son of your female servant.
     You have freed me from my chains.
17  I will bring a song of thanksgiving
        to you as a sacrifice.

I will call on the name of the LORD.
18 I will keep my vows to the LORD
in the presence of all his people,
19 in the courtyards of the LORD's house,
in the middle of Jerusalem.

Hallelujah!

## PSALM 117

1 Praise the LORD, all you nations!
Praise him, all you people of the world!
2 His mercy toward us is powerful.
The LORD's faithfulness endures forever.

Hallelujah!

## PROVERBS 24:10-22

10 If you faint in a crisis, you are weak.
11 Rescue captives condemned to death,
and spare those staggering toward their slaughter.
12 When you say, "We didn't know this,"
won't the one who weighs hearts take note of it?
Won't the one who guards your soul know it?
Won't he pay back people for what they do?

13 Eat honey, my son, because it is good.
Honey that flows from the honeycomb
tastes sweet.
14 The knowledge of wisdom is like that
for your soul.
If you find it, then there is a future,
and your hope will never be cut off.

<sup>15</sup> You wicked one,
>> do not lie in ambush at the home
>>> of a righteous person.
>> Do not rob his house.

<sup>16</sup>  A righteous person may fall seven times,
>>> but he gets up again.
>>>> However, in a disaster wicked people fall.

<sup>17</sup> Do not be happy when your enemy falls,
>> and do not feel glad when he stumbles.

<sup>18</sup>  The LORD will see it, he won't like it,
>>> and he will turn his anger away
>>>> from that person.

<sup>19</sup> Do not get overly upset with evildoers.
> Do not envy wicked people,

<sup>20</sup>  because an evil person has no future,
>> and the lamps of wicked people
>>> will be snuffed out.

<sup>21</sup> Fear the LORD, my son.
> Fear the king as well.
>> Do not associate with those who always insist
>>> upon change,

<sup>22</sup>  because disaster will come to them suddenly.
>> Who knows what misery both may bring?


# *Day 70* ❧

## PSALM 118

<sup>1</sup>  Give thanks to the LORD because he is good,
>> because his mercy endures forever.

2 Israel should say,
    "His mercy endures forever."
3 The descendants of Aaron should say,
    "His mercy endures forever."
4 Those who fear the LORD should say,
    "His mercy endures forever."

5 During times of trouble I called on the LORD.
    The LORD answered me ˌandˌ set me free
      ˌfrom all of themˌ.
6 The LORD is on my side.
    I am not afraid.
      What can mortals do to me?
7 The LORD is on my side as my helper.
    I will see ˌthe defeat ofˌ those who hate me.
8 It is better to depend on the LORD
    than to trust mortals.
9 It is better to depend on the LORD
    than to trust influential people.

10 All the nations surrounded me,
    ˌbut armedˌ with the name of the LORD,
      I defeated them.
11 They surrounded me. Yes, they surrounded me,
    ˌbut armedˌ with the name of the LORD,
      I defeated them.
12 They swarmed around me like bees,
    but they were extinguished like burning thornbushes.
      ˌSo armedˌ with the name of the LORD,
        I defeated them.
13 They pushed hard to make me fall,
    but the LORD helped me.
14 The LORD is my strength and my song.
    He is my savior.

15 The sound of joyful singing and victory is heard
    in the tents of righteous people.
      The right hand of the LORD displays strength.
16       The right hand of the LORD is held high.
      The right hand of the LORD displays strength.
17 I will not die,
    but I will live and tell what the LORD has done.
18 The LORD disciplined me severely,
    but he did not allow me to be killed.

19 Open the gates of righteousness for me.
    I will go through them ˌandˌ give thanks to the LORD.
20 This is the gate of the LORD
    through which righteous people will enter.

21 I give thanks to you,
    because you have answered me.
      You are my savior.
22 The stone that the builders rejected
    has become the cornerstone.
23 The LORD is responsible for this,
    and it is amazing for us to see.
24 This is the day the LORD has made.
    Let's rejoice and be glad today!
25 We beg you, O LORD, save us!
We beg you, O LORD, give us success!
26     Blessed is the one who comes in the name
      of the LORD.
    We bless you from the LORD's house.
27 The LORD is God, and he has given us light.
    March in a festival procession
      with branches to the horns of the altar.
28 You are my God, and I give thanks to you.
My God, I honor you highly.

29 Give thanks to the LORD because he is good,
  because his mercy endures forever.


## PROVERBS 24:23-34

*Learning From Wise People*

23 These also are the sayings of wise people:

  Showing partiality as a judge is not good.
24 Whoever says to a guilty person,
    "You are innocent,"
    will be cursed by people
      and condemned by nations.
25 But people will be pleased with those
    who convict a guilty person,
    and a great blessing will come to them.
26 Giving a straight answer is like a kiss on the lips.

27 Prepare your work outside,
    and get things ready for yourself in the field.
    Afterwards, build your house.

28 Do not testify against your neighbor
    without a reason,
    and do not deceive with your lips.
29 Do not say,
    "I'll treat him as he treated me.
    I'll pay him back for what he has done to me."

30 I passed by a lazy person's field,
    the vineyard belonging to a person without sense.
31 I saw that it was all overgrown with thistles.
    The ground was covered with weeds,
      and its stone fence was torn down.

32 When I observed ⸢this⸣, I took it to heart.
    I saw it and learned my lesson.
33 "Just a little sleep,
    just a little slumber,
    just a little nap."
34     Then your poverty will come like a drifter,
      and your need will come like a bandit.

# *Day 71* ➣

## PSALM 119[a]:1-24

1 Blessed are those whose lives have integrity,
    those who follow the teachings of the LORD.
2 Blessed are those who obey his written instructions.
    They wholeheartedly search for him.
3     They do nothing wrong.
    They follow his directions.
4 You have commanded
    that your guiding principles be carefully followed.
5 I pray that my ways may become firmly established
    so that I can obey your laws.
6     Then I will never feel ashamed
      when I study all your commandments.
7 I will give thanks to you
    as I learn your regulations, which are based
    on your righteousness.

---

[a] 119:1 Psalm 119 is a poem in Hebrew alphabetical order.

8   I will obey your laws.
      Never abandon me.

9   How can a young person keep his life pure?
      ⌊He can do it⌋ by holding on to your word.
10  I wholeheartedly searched for you.
      Do not let me wander away
        from your commandments.
11  I have treasured your promise in my heart
      so that I may not sin against you.
12  Thanks be to you, O LORD.
      Teach me your laws.
13  With my lips I have repeated
      every regulation that ⌊comes⌋ from your mouth.
14  I find joy in the way
        ⌊shown by⌋ your written instructions
      more than I find joy in all kinds of riches.
15  I want to reflect on your guiding principles
      and study your ways.
16  Your laws make me happy.
      I never forget your word.

17  Be kind to me so that I may live
      and hold on to your word.
18  Uncover my eyes
      so that I may see the miraculous things
        in your teachings.
19  I am a foreigner in this world.
      Do not hide your commandments from me.
20  My soul is overwhelmed with endless longing
        for your regulations.
21  You threaten arrogant people, who are condemned
      and wander away from your commandments.
22  Remove the insults and contempt

that have fallen on me
because I have obeyed your written instructions.
23 Even though influential people plot against me,
I reflect on your laws.
24 Indeed, your written instructions make me happy.
They are my best friends.

## PROVERBS 25:1-10

1 These also are Solomon's proverbs that were copied
by the men of King Hezekiah of Judah.

### Advice for Kings

2 It is the glory of God to hide things
but the glory of kings to investigate them.
3 ˌLikeˌ the high heavens and the deep earth,
so the mind of kings is unsearchable.
4 Take the impurities out of silver,
and a vessel is ready for the silversmith to mold.
5 Take a wicked person away from the presence
of a king,
and justice will make his throne secure.

6 Do not brag about yourself in front of a king
or stand in the spot that belongs
to notable people,
7 because it is better to be told, "Come up here,"
than to be put down in front of a prince
whom your eyes have seen.

8 Do not be in a hurry to go to court.
What will you do in the end
if your neighbor disgraces you?
9 Present your argument to your neighbor,
but do not reveal another person's secret.

10      Otherwise, when he hears about it,
              he will humiliate you,
          and his evil report about you
              will never disappear.

# *Day 72* ❧

## PSALM 119:25-48

25  I am close to death.
        Give me a new life as you promised.
26  I told you what I have done, and you answered me.
        Teach me your laws.
27    Help me understand your guiding principles
          so that I may reflect on your miracles.
28  I am drowning in tears.
        Strengthen me as you promised.
29  Turn me away from a life of lies.
        Graciously provide me with your teachings.
30  I have chosen a life of faithfulness.
    I have set your regulations in front of me.
31  I have clung tightly to your written instructions.
        O LORD, do not let me be put to shame.
32  I will eagerly pursue your commandments
        because you continue to increase
            my understanding.

33  Teach me, O LORD, how to live by your laws,
        and I will obey them to the end.
34  Help me understand so that I can follow
        your teachings.
        I will guard them with all my heart.

<sup>35</sup> Lead me on the path of your commandments,
   because I am happy with them.
<sup>36</sup> Direct my heart toward your written instructions
   rather than getting rich in underhanded ways.
<sup>37</sup> Turn my eyes away from worthless things.
   Give me a new life in your ways.
<sup>38</sup> Keep your promise to me
   so that I can fear you.
<sup>39</sup> Take away insults, which I dread,
   because your regulations are good.
<sup>40</sup> I long for your guiding principles.
   Give me a new life in your righteousness.

<sup>41</sup> Let your blessings reach me, O LORD.
   Save me as you promised.
<sup>42</sup>    Then I will have an answer
         for the one who insults me
      since I trust your word.
<sup>43</sup> Do not take so much as a single word of truth
      from my mouth.
   My hope is based on your regulations.
<sup>44</sup> I will follow your teachings forever and ever.
<sup>45</sup> I will walk around freely
      because I sought out your guiding principles.
<sup>46</sup> I will speak about your written instructions
      in the presence of kings
      and not feel ashamed.
<sup>47</sup> Your commandments, which I love,
      make me happy.
<sup>48</sup> I lift my hands in prayer
      because of your commandments,
   which I love.
   I will reflect on your laws.

## PROVERBS 25:11-20

11  Like golden apples in silver settings,
     so is a word spoken at the right time.
12  Like a gold ring and a fine gold ornament,
     so is constructive criticism to the ear of one
          who listens.
13  Like the coolness of snow on a harvest day,
     so is a trustworthy messenger to those
          who send him:
     He refreshes his masters.
14  Like a dense fog or a dust storm,
     so is a person who brags about a gift
          that he does not give.

15  With patience you can persuade a ruler,
     and a soft tongue can break bones.
16  When you find honey,
          eat only as much as you need.
     Otherwise, you will have too much and vomit.
17  Do not set foot in your neighbor's house too often.
     Otherwise, he will see too much of you
          and hate you.

18  Like a club and a sword and a sharp arrow,
     so is a person who gives false testimony
          against his neighbor.
19  Like a broken tooth and a lame foot,
     so is confidence in an unfaithful person
          in a time of crisis.
20  Like taking off a coat on a cold day
     or pouring vinegar on baking soda,
          so is singing songs to one who has
               an evil heart.

# Day 73 ≈

### PSALM 119:49-72

49 Remember the word you gave me.
  Through it you gave me hope.
50 This is my comfort in my misery:
  Your promise gave me a new life.
51 Arrogant people have mocked me with cruelty,
  yet I have not turned away from your teachings.
52 I remembered your regulations from long ago, O LORD,
  and I found comfort in them.
53 I am burning with anger because of wicked people,
  who abandon your teachings.
54 Your laws have become like psalms to me
  in this place where I am only a foreigner.
55 At night I remember your name, O LORD,
  and I follow your teachings.
56 This has happened to me
  because I have obeyed your guiding principles.

57 You are my inheritance, O LORD.
  I promised to hold on to your words.
58 With all my heart I want to win your favor.
  Be kind to me as you promised.
59 I have thought about my life,
  and I have directed my feet back
    to your written instructions.
60 Without any hesitation I hurry to obey
    your commandments.
61 Though the ropes of wicked people
    are tied around me,

I never forget your teachings.
62 At midnight I wake up to give thanks to you
for the regulations, which are based
on your righteousness.
63 I am a friend to everyone who fears you
and to everyone who follows
your guiding principles.
64 Your mercy, O LORD, fills the earth.
Teach me your laws.

65 You have treated me well, O LORD,
as you promised.
66 Teach me ˌto useˌ good judgment and knowledge,
because I believe in your commandments.
67 Before you made me suffer, I used to wander off,
but now I hold on to your word.
68 You are good, and you do good things.
Teach me your laws.
69 Arrogant people have smeared me with lies,
ˌyetˌ I obey your guiding principles
with all my heart.
70 Their hearts are cold and insensitive,
ˌyetˌ I am happy with your teachings.
71 It was good that I had to suffer
in order to learn your laws.
72 The teachings ˌthat comeˌ from your mouth
are worth more to me
than thousands in gold or silver.

## PROVERBS 25:21-28

21 If your enemy is hungry, give him some food to eat,
and if he is thirsty, give him some water to drink.

22        ⌊In this way⌋ you will make him feel guilty
           and ashamed,
           and the LORD will reward you.

23   ⌊As⌋ the north wind brings rain,
       so a whispering tongue brings angry looks.

24   Better to live on a corner of a roof
       than to share a home with a quarreling woman.

25   ⌊Like⌋ cold water to a thirsty soul,
       so is good news from far away.

26   ⌊Like⌋ a muddied spring and a polluted well,
       ⌊so⌋ is a righteous person who gives in
           to a wicked person.

27   Eating too much honey is not good,
       and searching for honor is not honorable.[a]

28   ⌊Like⌋ a city broken into ⌊and⌋ left without a wall,
       ⌊so⌋ is a person who lacks self-control.

# Day 74 ≈

## PSALM 119:73-96

73   Your hands created me and made me what I am.
       Help me understand so that I may learn
           your commandments.

74   Those who fear you will see me and rejoice,
       because my hope is based on your word.

75   I know that your regulations are fair, O LORD,
       and that you were right to make me suffer.

---

[a] 25:27 Hebrew meaning of this line uncertain.

**76** Let your mercy comfort me
as you promised.
**77** Let your compassion reach me so that I may live,
because your teachings make me happy.
**78** Let arrogant people be put to shame
because they lied about me,
˳yet˳ I reflect on your guiding principles.
**79** Let those who fear you turn to me
so that they can come to know
your written instructions.
**80** Let my heart be filled with integrity
in regard to your laws
so that I will not be put to shame.

**81** My soul is weak from waiting for you to save me.
My hope is based on your word.
**82** My eyes have become strained from looking
for your promise.
I ask, "When will you comfort me?"
**83** Although I have become like a shriveled
and dried out wineskin,
I have not forgotten your laws.
**84** What is left of my life?
When will you bring those who persecute me to justice?
**85** Arrogant people have dug pits to trap me
in defiance of your teachings.
**86** (All your commandments are reliable.)
Those people persecute me with lies. Help me!
**87** They almost wiped me off ˳the face of˳ the earth.
But I did not abandon your guiding principles.
**88** Give me a new life through your mercy
so that I may obey the written instructions,
˳which came˳ from your mouth.

**89**    O LORD, your word is established in heaven forever.
**90**      Your faithfulness endures
       throughout every generation.
    You set the earth in place,
      and it continues to stand.
**91**       All things continue to stand today
       because of your regulations,
     since they are all your servants.
**92**    If your teachings had not made me happy,
     then I would have died in my misery.
**93**    I will never forget your guiding principles,
     because you gave me a new life through them.
**94**    I am yours.
     Save me, because I have searched
      for your guiding principles.
**95**    The wicked people have waited for me
     in order to destroy me,
    ⌊yet⌋ I want to understand your written instructions.
**96**    I have seen a limit to everything else,
    ⌊but⌋ your commandments have no limit.

## PROVERBS 26:1-12

### All About Fools

**1**    Like snow in summertime and rain at harvest time,
     so honor is not right for a fool.
**2**    Like a fluttering sparrow,
   like a darting swallow,
     so a hastily spoken curse does not come to rest.
**3**    A whip is for the horse,
    a bridle is for the donkey,
      and a rod is for the backs of fools.

⁴ Do not answer a fool with his own stupidity,
    or you will be like him.
⁵ Answer a fool with his own stupidity,
    or he will think he is wise.
⁶ Whoever uses a fool to send a message
    cuts off his own feet and brings violence
        upon himself.

⁷ ⌊Like⌋ a lame person's limp legs,
    so is a proverb in the mouths of fools.
⁸ Like tying a stone to a sling,
    so is giving honor to a fool.
⁹ ⌊Like⌋ a thorn stuck in a drunk's hand,
    so is a proverb in the mouths of fools.
¹⁰ ⌊Like⌋ many people who destroy everything,
    so is one who hires fools or drifters.
¹¹ As a dog goes back to its vomit,
    ⌊so⌋ a fool repeats his stupidity.
¹² Have you met a person who thinks he is wise?
    There is more hope for a fool than for him.

# *Day 75* ❦

## PSALM 119:97-120

⁹⁷ Oh, how I love your teachings!
    They are in my thoughts all day long.
⁹⁸ Your commandments make me wiser
        than my enemies,
    because your commandments are always
        with me.

99 I have more insight than all my teachers,
    because your written instructions
        are in my thoughts.

100 I have more wisdom than those with many years
        of experience,
    because I have obeyed your guiding principles.

101 I have kept my feet from walking on any evil path
    in order to obey your word.

102 I have not neglected your regulations,
    because you have taught me.

103 How sweet the taste of your promise is!
    It tastes sweeter than honey.

104 From your guiding principles I gain understanding.
    That is why I hate every path that leads to lying.

105 Your word is a lamp for my feet
    and a light for my path.

106 I took an oath, and I will keep it.
    I took an oath to follow your regulations,
        which are based on your righteousness.

107 I have suffered so much.
    Give me a new life, O LORD, as you promised.

108 Please accept the praise I gladly give you, O LORD,
    and teach me your regulations.

109 I always take my life into my own hands,
    but I never forget your teachings.

110 Wicked people have set a trap for me,
    but I have never wandered away
        from your guiding principles.

111 Your written instructions are mine forever.
    They are the joy of my heart.

112 I have decided to obey your laws.
    They offer a reward that never ends.

113 I hate two-faced people,
   but I love your teachings.
114 You are my hiding place and my shield.
   My hope is based on your word.
115 Get away from me, you evildoers,
   so that I can obey the commandments
      of my God.
116 Help me God, as you promised, so that I may live.
   Do not turn my hope into disappointment.
117 Hold me, and I will be safe,
   and I will always respect your laws.
118 You reject all who wander away from your laws,
   because their lies mislead them.ᵃ
119 You get rid of all wicked people on earth
   as if they were rubbish.
   That is why I love your written instructions.
120 My body shudders in fear of you,
   and I am afraid of your regulations.

## PROVERBS 26:13-19

13 A lazy person says,
   "There's a ferocious lion out on the road!
   There's a lion loose in the streets!"
14 ⌊As⌋ a door turns on its hinges,
   so the lazy person turns on his bed.
15 A lazy person puts his fork in his food.
   He wears himself out as he brings it back
      to his mouth.
16 A lazy person thinks he is wiser than seven people
   who give a sensible answer.

---

ᵃ 119:118 Hebrew meaning of this line uncertain.

17   ⌊Like⌋ grabbing a dog by the ears,
        ⌊so⌋ is a bystander who gets involved
           in someone else's quarrel.
18   Like a madman who shoots flaming arrows,
        arrows, and death,
19      so is the person who tricks his neighbor
           and says, "I was only joking!"

# *Day 76* ≈

## PSALM 119:121-144

121  I have done what is fair and right.
        Do not leave me at the mercy
           of those who oppress me.
122  Guarantee my well-being.
        Do not let arrogant people oppress me.
123  My eyes are strained from looking for you
           to save me
        and from looking for the fulfillment
           of your righteous promise.
124  Treat me with kindness,
        and teach me your laws.
125  I am your servant.
        Help me understand
           so that I may come to know
              your written instructions.
126  It is time for you to act, O Lord.[a]
        Even though people have abolished
           your teachings,

---

[a] 119:126 One Hebrew manuscript, Latin; other Hebrew manuscripts "It is time to act for the Lord."

127       I love your commandments more than gold,
          more than pure gold.
128       I follow the straight paths
          of your guiding principles.
      I hate every pathway that leads to lying.

129   Your written instructions are miraculous.
      That is why I obey them.
130   Your word is a doorway that lets in light,
      and it helps gullible people understand.
131   I open my mouth and pant
      because I long for your commandments.
132   Turn toward me, and have pity on me
      as you have pledged to do for those
          who love your name.
133   Make my steps secure through your promise,
      and do not let any sin control me.
134   Save me from human oppression
      so that I may obey your guiding principles.
135   Smile on me,
      and teach me your laws.
136   Streams of tears flow from my eyes
      because others do not follow your teachings.

137   You are righteous, O LORD,
      and your regulations are fair.
138   You have issued your written instructions.
      They are fair and completely dependable.
139   My devotion for your words consumes me,
      because my enemies have forgotten your words.
140   Your promise has been thoroughly tested,
      and I love it.
141   I am unimportant and despised,
      yet I never forget your guiding principles.

<sup>142</sup> Your righteousness is an everlasting righteousness,
    and your teachings are reliable.
<sup>143</sup> Trouble and hardship have found me,
    but your commandments ˌstillˌ make me happy.
<sup>144</sup> Your written instructions are always right.
    Help me understand ˌthemˌ so that I will live.


### PROVERBS 26:20-28

<sup>20</sup> Without wood a fire goes out,
    and without gossip a quarrel dies down.
<sup>21</sup>   ˌAsˌ charcoal fuels burning coals
      and wood fuels fire,
    so a quarrelsome person fuels a dispute.
<sup>22</sup>   The words of a gossip are swallowed greedily,
    and they go down
      into a person's innermost being.

<sup>23</sup> ˌLikeˌ a clay pot covered with cheap silver,
    ˌsoˌ is smooth talk that covers up an evil heart.
<sup>24</sup> Whoever is filled with hate disguises it
    with his speech,
  but inside he holds on to deceit.
<sup>25</sup>   When he talks charmingly, do not trust him
    because of the seven disgusting things
      in his heart.
<sup>26</sup>   His hatred is deceitfully hidden,
    but his wickedness will be revealed
      to the community.

<sup>27</sup> Whoever digs a pit will fall into it.
Whoever rolls a stone will have it roll back on him.
<sup>28</sup>   A lying tongue hates its victims,
    and a flattering mouth causes ruin.

# Day 77 ≈

## PSALM 119:145-176

¹⁴⁵ I have called out with all my heart. Answer me,
O LORD.
I want to obey your laws.
¹⁴⁶ I have called out.
Save me, so that I can obey your written instructions.
¹⁴⁷ I got up before dawn, and I cried out for help.
My hope is based on your word.
¹⁴⁸ My eyes are wide-open
throughout the nighttime hours
to reflect on your word.
¹⁴⁹ In keeping with your mercy, hear my voice.
O LORD, give me a new life guided by your regulations.
¹⁵⁰ Those who carry out plots against me are near,
˻yet˼ they are far away from your teachings.
¹⁵¹ You are near, O LORD,
and all your commandments are reliable.
¹⁵² Long ago I learned from your written instructions
that you made them to last forever.

¹⁵³ Look at my misery, and rescue me,
because I have never forgotten your teachings.
¹⁵⁴ Plead my case ˻for me˼, and save me.
Give me a new life as you promised.
¹⁵⁵ Wicked people are far from being saved,
because they have not searched for your laws.
¹⁵⁶ Your acts of compassion are many in number,
O LORD.
Give me a new life guided by your regulations.

157 I have many persecutors and opponents,
   ⌐yet⌐ I have not turned away
       from your written instructions.

158 I have seen traitors,
   and I am filled with disgust.
      They have not accepted your promise.

159 See how I have loved your guiding principles!
   O LORD, in keeping with your mercy,
      give me a new life.

160 There is nothing but truth in your word,
   and all of your righteous regulations
      endure forever.


161 Influential people have persecuted me
      for no reason,
   but it is only your words that fill my heart
      with terror.

162 I find joy in your promise
   like someone who finds a priceless treasure.

163 I hate lying; I am disgusted with it.
   I love your teachings.

164 Seven times a day I praise you
   for your righteous regulations.

165 There is lasting peace for those
      who love your teachings.
   Nothing can make those people stumble.

166 I have waited with hope for you to save me, O LORD.
   I have carried out your commandments.

167 I have obeyed your written instructions.
   I have loved them very much.

168 I have followed your guiding principles
      and your written instructions,
   because my whole life is in front of you.

169 Let my cry for help come into your presence,
O LORD.
Help me understand as you promised.
170 Let my plea for mercy come into your presence.
Rescue me as you promised.
171 Let my lips pour out praise
because you teach me your laws.
172 Let my tongue sing about your promise
because all your commandments are fair.
173 Let your hand help me
because I have chosen to follow
your guiding principles.
174 I have longed for you to save me, O LORD,
and your teachings make me happy.
175 Let my soul have new life so that it can praise you.
Let your regulations help me.
176 I have wandered away like a lost lamb.
Search for me,
because I have never forgotten
your commandments.

## PROVERBS 27:1-14

### All About Life

1 Do not brag about tomorrow,
because you do not know
what another day may bring.
2 Praise should come from another person
and not from your own mouth,
from a stranger and not from your own lips.
3 A stone is heavy, and sand weighs a lot,
but annoyance caused by a stubborn fool
is heavier than both.

4   Anger is cruel, and fury is overwhelming,
     but who can survive jealousy?

5   Open criticism is better than unexpressed love.
6   Wounds made by a friend are intended to help,
     but an enemy's kisses are too much to bear.[a]
7   One who is full despises honey,
     but to one who is hungry,
       even bitter food tastes sweet.
8   Like a bird wandering from its nest,
     so is a husband wandering from his home.

9   Perfume and incense make the heart glad,
     but the sweetness of a friend is a fragrant forest.[b]
10   Do not abandon your friend or your father's friend.
     Do not go to a relative's home when you are
       in trouble.
     A neighbor living nearby is better
       than a relative far away.

11   Be wise, my son, and make my heart glad
     so that I can answer anyone who criticizes me.
12   Sensible people foresee trouble and hide.
     Gullible people go ahead ˌandˌ suffer.
13      Hold on to the garment of one
       who guarantees a stranger's loan,
     and hold responsible the person
       who makes a loan in behalf of a foreigner.
14   Whoever blesses his friend early in the morning
     with a loud voice—
       his blessing is considered a curse.

---

[a] 27:6 Hebrew meaning of "are too much to bear" uncertain.    [b] 27:9 Or "is sincere advice."

# Day 78 ⁂

## PSALM 120

A song for going up to worship.

1 When I was in trouble, I cried out to the LORD,
   and he answered me.
2 O LORD, rescue me from lying lips
   and from a deceitful tongue.

3 You deceitful tongue, what can the LORD give you?
   What more can he do for you?
4     He will give you a warrior's sharpened arrows
      and red-hot coals.

5 How horrible it is to live as a foreigner in Meshech
   or to stay in the tents of Kedar.
6     I have lived too long with those who hate peace.
7     I am for peace, but when I talk about it,
      they only talk about war.

## PSALM 121

A song for going up to worship.

1 I look up toward the mountains.
   Where can I find help?
2 My help comes from the LORD,
   the maker of heaven and earth.
3 He will not let you fall.
   Your guardian will not fall asleep.
4 Indeed, the Guardian of Israel never rests or sleeps.
5 The LORD is your guardian.

The LORD is the shade over your right hand.
6      The sun will not beat down on you during the day,
           nor will the moon at night.
7   The LORD guards you from every evil.
        He guards your life.
8   The LORD guards you as you come and go,
        now and forever.


## PSALM 122

A song by David for going up to worship.

1   I was glad when they said to me,
        "Let's go to the house of the LORD."
2   Our feet are standing inside your gates, Jerusalem.
3   Jerusalem is built to be a city
        where the people are united.[a]
4   All of the LORD's tribes go to that city
           because it is a law in Israel
               to give thanks to the name of the LORD.
5   The court of justice sits there.
        It consists of ⌞princes
               who are⌟ David's descendants.

6   Pray for the peace of Jerusalem:
        "May those who love you prosper.
7          May there be peace inside your walls
               and prosperity in your palaces."
8   For the sake of my relatives and friends, let me say,
        "May it go well for you!"
9   For the sake of the house of the LORD our God,
        I will seek what is good for you.

---

[a] 122:3 Hebrew meaning of this verse uncertain.

## PROVERBS 27:15-27

<sup>15</sup> Constantly dripping water on a rainy day is like
a quarreling woman.
<sup>16</sup> Whoever can control her can control the wind.
He can even pick up olive oil
with his right hand.<sup>a</sup>

<sup>17</sup> ˻As˼ iron sharpens iron,
so one person sharpens the wits of another.
<sup>18</sup> Whoever takes care of a fig tree can eat its fruit,
and whoever protects his master is honored.
<sup>19</sup> As a face is reflected in water,
so a person is reflected by his heart.
<sup>20</sup> Hell and decay are never satisfied,
and a person's eyes are never satisfied.

<sup>21</sup> The crucible is for refining silver
and the smelter for gold,
but a person ˻is tested˼ by the praise given to him.
<sup>22</sup> If you crush a stubborn fool in a mortar with a pestle
along with grain,<sup>b</sup>
˻even then˼ his stupidity will not leave him.
<sup>23</sup> Be fully aware of the condition of your flock,
and pay close attention to your herds.
<sup>24</sup> Wealth is not forever.
Nor does a crown last
from one generation to the next.

<sup>25</sup> ˻When˼ grass is cut short, the tender growth appears,
and vegetables are gathered on the hills.
<sup>26</sup> Lambs ˻will provide˼ you with clothing,
and the money from the male goats
will buy a field.

---

<sup>a</sup> 27:16 Hebrew meaning of this line uncertain.  <sup>b</sup> 27:22 Hebrew meaning uncertain.

27      There will be enough goat milk
                to feed you,
            to feed your family,
                and to keep your servant girls alive.

# *Day 79* ≈

## PSALM 123

A song for going up to worship.

1   I look up to you,
        to the one who sits enthroned in heaven.
2   As servants depend on their masters,
    as a maid depends on her mistress,
        so we depend on the LORD our God
            until he has pity on us.
3   Have pity on us, O LORD.
    Have pity on us
        because we have suffered more than our share
            of contempt.
4   We have suffered more than our share of ridicule
        from those who are carefree.
    We have suffered more than our share of contempt
        from those who are arrogant.

## PSALM 124

A song by David for going up to worship.

1   "If the LORD had not been on our side. . ."
        (Israel should repeat this.)
2   "If the LORD had not been on our side
        when people attacked us,

3 then they would have swallowed us alive
   when their anger exploded against us.
4 Then the floodwaters would have swept us away.
   An ˎoverflowingˏ stream
     would have washed us away.
5 Then raging water would have washed us away."

6 Thank the LORD, who did not let them
   sink their teeth into us.
7 We escaped like a bird caught in a hunter's trap.
   The trap was broken, and we escaped.
8 Our help is in the name of the LORD,
   the maker of heaven and earth.

## PSALM 125

A song for going up to worship.

1 Those who trust the LORD are like Mount Zion,
   which can never be shaken.
    It remains firm forever.
2 ˎAsˏ the mountains surround Jerusalem,
   so the LORD surrounds his people
    now and forever.

3 A wicked ruler will not be allowed to govern
   the land set aside for righteous people.
    That is why righteous people do not use
     their power to do wrong.

4 Do good, O LORD, to those who are good,
   to those whose motives are decent.
5 But when people become crooked,
   the LORD will lead them away with troublemakers.

  Let there be peace in Israel!

## PSALM 126

A song for going up to worship.

1 When the LORD restored the fortunes of Zion,
   it was as if we were dreaming.
2 Then our mouths were filled with laughter
   and our tongues with joyful songs.
   Then the nations said,
   "The LORD has done spectacular things for them."

3 The LORD has done spectacular things for us.
   We are overjoyed.
4 Restore our fortunes, O LORD,
   as you restore streams ˌto dry riverbedsˌ
   in the Negev.
5 Those who cry while they plant
   will joyfully sing while they harvest.
6 The person who goes out weeping,
   carrying his bag of seed,
   will come home singing,
   carrying his bundles of grain.

## PROVERBS 28:1-10

1 A wicked person flees when no one is chasing him,
   but righteous people are as bold as lions.
2 When a country is in revolt, it has many rulers,
   but only with a person who has understanding
   and knowledge
   will it last a long time.
3 A poor person who oppresses poorer people
   is like a driving rain that leaves no food.
4 Those who abandon ˌGod'sˌ teachings praise
   wicked people,

but those who follow ⸜God's⸝ teachings oppose
wicked people.
5    Evil people do not understand justice,
but those who seek the LORD
understand everything.
6    Better to be a poor person who has integrity
than to be rich and double-dealing.

7    Whoever follows ⸜God's⸝ teachings is a wise son.
Whoever associates with gluttons disgraces
his father.
8    Whoever becomes wealthy through ⸜unfair⸝ loans
and interest
collects them for the one who is kind to the poor.
9    Surely the prayer of someone who refuses
to listen to ⸜God's⸝ teachings is disgusting.
10   Whoever leads decent people into evil will fall
into his own pit,
but innocent people will inherit good things.


# *Day 80* ❧

## PSALM 127

A song by Solomon for going up to worship.

1    If the LORD does not build the house,
it is useless for the builders to work on it.
If the LORD does not protect a city,
it is useless for the guard to stay alert.
2        It is useless to work hard for the food you eat
by getting up early and going to bed late.

The LORD gives food to those he loves
while they sleep.

3 Children are an inheritance from the LORD.
They are a reward from him.
4   The children born to a man when he is young
are like arrows in the hand of a warrior.
5     Blessed is the man who has filled his quiver
with them.
He will not be put to shame
when he speaks with his enemies
in the city gate.


## PSALM 128

A song for going up to worship.

1 Blessed are all who fear the LORD
and live his way.

2 You will certainly eat what your own hands
have provided.
Blessings to you!
May things go well for you!
3 Your wife will be like a fruitful vine inside your home.
Your children will be like young olive trees
around your table.
4   This is how the LORD will bless the person
who fears him.
5     May the LORD bless you from Zion
so that you may see Jerusalem prospering
all the days of your life.
6     May you live to see your children's children.

Let there be peace in Israel!

## PSALM 129

A song for going up to worship.

1   "From the time I was young,
        people have attacked me. . ."
      (Israel should repeat this.)
2   "From the time I was young,
        people have attacked me,
      but they have never overpowered me.
3       They have plowed my back
            ⌊like farmers plow fields⌋.
        They made long slashes ⌊like furrows⌋."
4   The LORD is righteous.
      He has cut me loose
        from the ropes that wicked people
            tied around me.
5   Put to shame all those who hate Zion.
      Force them to retreat.
6     Make them be like grass on a roof,
        like grass that dries up before it produces a stalk.
7         It will never fill the barns of those who harvest
            or the arms of those who gather bundles.
8           Those who pass by
              will never say ⌊to them⌋,
            "May you be blessed by the LORD"
              or "We bless you in the name
                of the LORD."

## PSALM 130

A song for going up to worship.

1   O LORD, out of the depths I call to you.
2   O Lord, hear my voice.

Let your ears be open to my pleas for mercy.

3   O LORD, who would be able to stand
      if you kept a record of sins?

4   But with you there is forgiveness
      so that you can be feared.

5   I wait for the LORD, my soul waits,
      and with hope I wait for his word.

6   My soul waits for the LORD
      more than those who watch for the morning,
      more than those who watch for the morning.

7   O Israel, put your hope in the LORD,
      because with the LORD there is mercy
        and with him there is unlimited forgiveness.

8         He will rescue Israel from all its sins.

## PROVERBS 28:11-19

11   A rich person is wise in his own eyes,
      but a poor person with understanding
        sees right through him.

12   When righteous people triumph, there is great glory,
      but when wicked people rise,
        people hide themselves.

13   Whoever covers over his sins does not prosper.
    Whoever confesses and abandons them
      receives compassion.

14   Blessed is the one who is always fearful ˌof sinˌ,
      but whoever is hard-hearted falls into disaster.

15   ˌLikeˌ a roaring lion and a charging bear,
      ˌsoˌ a wicked ruler is a threat to poor people.

16   A leader without understanding taxes
      ˌhis peopleˌ heavily,
      but those who hate unjust gain will live longer.

<sup>17</sup> A person burdened with the guilt of murder
　　　will be a fugitive down to his grave.
　　　　　No one will help him.

<sup>18</sup> Whoever lives honestly will be safe.
　　Whoever lives dishonestly will fall all at once.
<sup>19</sup> Whoever works his land will have plenty to eat.
　　Whoever chases unrealistic dreams will have
　　　　　plenty of nothing.


# *Day 81* ＊

## PSALM 131

A song by David for going up to worship.

<sup>1</sup> O LORD, my heart is not conceited.
　　My eyes do not look down on others.
　　I am not involved in things too big
　　　　or too difficult for me.
<sup>2</sup> Instead, I have kept my soul calm and quiet.
　　My soul is content as a weaned child is content
　　　　in its mother's arms.
<sup>3</sup> Israel, put your hope in the LORD now and forever.


## PSALM 132

A song for going up to worship.

<sup>1</sup> O LORD, remember David
　　　and all the hardships he endured.
<sup>2</sup> 　Remember how he swore an oath to the LORD
　　　　and made this vow to the Mighty One of Jacob:

<sup>3</sup>          "I will not step inside my house,
<sup>4</sup>             get into my bed, shut my eyes,
               or close my eyelids
<sup>5</sup>             until I find a place for the L<small>ORD</small>,
               a dwelling place for the Mighty One
                  of Jacob."

<sup>6</sup>  Now, we have heard about the ark of the promise
       being in Ephrathah.
       We have found it in Jaar.
<sup>7</sup>  Let's go to his dwelling place.
       Let's worship at his footstool.
<sup>8</sup>  O L<small>ORD</small>, arise, and come to your resting place
       with the ark of your power.
<sup>9</sup>  Clothe your priests with righteousness.
       Let your godly ones sing with joy.
<sup>10</sup> For the sake of your servant David,
       do not reject your anointed one.
<sup>11</sup> The L<small>ORD</small> swore an oath to David.
       This is a truth he will not take back:
          "I will set one of your own descendants
             on your throne.
<sup>12</sup>         If your sons are faithful to my promise[a]
           and my written instructions
             that I will teach them,
         then their descendants will also sit
           on your throne forever."

<sup>13</sup> The L<small>ORD</small> has chosen Zion.
       He wants it for his home.
<sup>14</sup>     "This will be my resting place forever.

---

[a] 132:12 Or "covenant."

Here I will sit enthroned because I want Zion.
15    I will certainly bless all that Zion needs.
I will satisfy its needy people with food.
16    I will clothe its priests with salvation.
Then its godly ones will sing joyfully.
17  There I will make a horn sprout up for David.
I will prepare a lamp for my anointed one.
18    I will clothe his enemies with shame,
but the crown on my anointed one will shine."

## PSALM 133

A song by David for going up to worship.

1   See how good and pleasant it is
when brothers and sisters live
together in harmony!
2       It is like fine, scented oil on the head,
running down the beard—
down Aaron's beard—
running over the collar of his robes.
3       It is like dew on ⌊Mount⌋ Hermon,
dew which comes down on Zion's mountains.
That is where the LORD promised
the blessing of eternal life.

## PSALM 134

A song for going up to worship.

1   Praise the LORD, all you servants of the LORD,
all who stand in the house of the LORD
night after night.

2   Lift your hands toward the holy place,
      and praise the LORD.

3   May the LORD, the maker of heaven and earth,
      bless you from Zion.

## PROVERBS 28:20-28

20   A trustworthy person has many blessings,
      but anyone in a hurry to get rich
        will not escape punishment.

21   Showing partiality is not good,
      because some people will turn on you even
        for a piece of bread.

22   A stingy person is in a hurry to get rich,
      not realizing that poverty
        is about to overtake him.

23   Whoever criticizes people will be
      more highly regarded in the future
      than the one who flatters with his tongue.

24   The one who robs his father or his mother
      and says, "It isn't wrong!" is a companion
        to a vandal.

25   A greedy person stirs up a fight,
      but whoever trusts the LORD prospers.

26   Whoever trusts his own heart is a fool.
      Whoever walks in wisdom will survive.

27   Whoever gives to the poor lacks nothing.
      Whoever ignores the poor receives many curses.

28   When wicked people rise, people hide.
      When they die, righteous people increase.

# Day 82 ～

## PSALM 135

1 Hallelujah!

Praise the name of the LORD.
Praise him, you servants of the LORD
2     who are standing in the house of the LORD,
        in the courtyards of the house of our God.
3 Praise the LORD because he is good.
Make music to praise his name
        because his name is beautiful.
4     The LORD chose Jacob to be his own
        and chose Israel to be his own special treasure.

5     I know that the LORD is great,
        that our Lord is greater than all the false gods.
6 The LORD does whatever he wants in heaven
        or on earth,
    on the seas or in all the depths of the oceans.
7 He is the one who makes the clouds rise
        from the ends of the earth,
    who makes lightning for the thunderstorms,
        and who brings wind out of his storerooms.

8 He is the one who killed every firstborn male
        in Egypt.
    He killed humans and animals alike.
9 He sent miraculous signs and amazing things
        into the heart of Egypt
    against Pharaoh and all his officials.
10 He is the one who defeated many nations

and killed mighty kings:

11     King Sihon of the Amorites,
King Og of Bashan,
    and all the kingdoms in Canaan.

12       He gave their land as an inheritance,
      an inheritance to his people Israel.

13   O LORD, your name endures forever.
O LORD, you will be remembered
    throughout every generation.

14     The LORD will provide justice for his people
    and have compassion on his servants.

15   The idols of the nations are made of silver and gold.
    They were made by human hands.[a]

16     They have mouths, but they cannot speak.
    They have eyes, but they cannot see.

17     They have ears, but they cannot hear.
    They cannot breathe.

18   Those who make idols end up like them.
    So does everyone who trusts them.

19   Descendants of Israel, praise the LORD.
Descendants of Aaron, praise the LORD.

20   Descendants of Levi, praise the LORD.
    You people who fear the LORD, praise the LORD.

21     Thank the LORD in Zion.
    Thank the one who lives in Jerusalem.

Hallelujah!

## PROVERBS 29:1-8

1   A person who will not bend after many warnings
    will suddenly be broken beyond repair.

---

[a] 135:15 Verses 15-18 are virtually identical in wording to Psalm 115:4-8.

2 When righteous people increase,
   the people ˌof Godˌ rejoice,
      but when a wicked person rules, everybody groans.
3 A person who loves wisdom makes his father happy,
   but one who pays prostitutes wastes his wealth.
4 By means of justice, a king builds up a country,
   but a person
      who confiscates religious contributions
      tears it down.

5 A person who flatters his neighbor
   is spreading a net for him to step into.
6 To an evil person sin is bait in a trap,
   but a righteous person runs away from it[a]
      and is glad.
7 A righteous person knows the just cause of the poor.
   A wicked person does not understand this.
8 Mockers create an uproar in a city,
   but wise people turn away anger.

# *Day 83* ❧

## PSALM 136

1 Give thanks to the LORD because he is good,
      because his mercy endures forever.
2 Give thanks to the God of gods
      because his mercy endures forever.

---

[a] 29:6 Hebrew meaning of "runs away from it" uncertain.

³   Give thanks to the Lord of lords
       because his mercy endures forever.

⁴   Give thanks to the only one
     who does miraculous things—
       because his mercy endures forever.
⁵     to the one who made the heavens
     by his understanding—
       because his mercy endures forever.
⁶     to the one who spread out the earth
     on the water—
       because his mercy endures forever.
⁷     to the one who made the great lights—
       because his mercy endures forever.
⁸     the sun to rule the day—
       because his mercy endures forever.
⁹     the moon and stars to rule the night—
       because his mercy endures forever.

¹⁰   Give thanks to the one
     who killed the firstborn males in Egypt—
       because his mercy endures forever.
¹¹     He brought Israel out from among them—
       because his mercy endures forever.
¹²     with a mighty hand and a powerful arm—
       because his mercy endures forever.

¹³   Give thanks to one who divided the Red Sea—
       because his mercy endures forever.
¹⁴     He led Israel through the middle of it—
       because his mercy endures forever.
¹⁵     He swept Pharaoh and his army
     into the Red Sea—
       because his mercy endures forever.

16 Give thanks to the one who led his people
       through the desert—
              because his mercy endures forever.

17 Give thanks to the one who defeated powerful kings—
              because his mercy endures forever.

18 He killed mighty kings—
              because his mercy endures forever.

19 King Sihon of the Amorites—
              because his mercy endures forever.

20 and King Og of Bashan—
              because his mercy endures forever.

21 He gave their land as an inheritance—
              because his mercy endures forever.

22 as an inheritance for his servant Israel—
              because his mercy endures forever.

23 He remembered us when we were humiliated—
              because his mercy endures forever.

24 He snatched us from the grasp of our enemies—
              because his mercy endures forever.

25 He gives food to every living creature—
              because his mercy endures forever.

26 Give thanks to the God of heaven
              because his mercy endures forever.

## PROVERBS 29:9-17

9 When a wise person goes to court
       with a stubborn fool,
   he may rant and rave,
       but there is no peace and quiet.

10 Bloodthirsty people hate an innocent person,
       but decent people seek ˌto protectˌ his life.

11 A fool expresses all his emotions,
   but a wise person controls them.
12 If a ruler pays attention to lies,
   all his servants become wicked.

13 A poor person and an oppressor have this
      in common:
   The LORD gives both of them sight.
14 When a king judges the poor with honesty,
   his throne will always be secure.

15 A spanking and a warning produce wisdom,
   but an undisciplined child disgraces his mother.
16 When wicked people increase, crime increases,
   but righteous people will witness their downfall.
17 Correct your son, and he will give you peace
      of mind.
   He will bring delight to your soul.


# *Day 84* ≈

## PSALM 137

1 By the rivers of Babylon, we sat down and cried
   as we remembered Zion.
2 We hung our lyres on willow trees.
3 It was there that those who had captured us
      demanded that we sing.
   Those who guarded us wanted us
      to entertain them.
      ⌐They said,⌐ "Sing a song from Zion for us!"

⁴ How could we sing the LORD's song
   in a foreign land?
⁵ If I forget you, Jerusalem,
   let my right hand forget ˹how to play the lyre˺.
⁶ Let my tongue stick to the roof of my mouth
   if I don't remember you,
   if I don't consider Jerusalem my highest joy.

⁷ O LORD, remember the people of Edom.
   Remember what they did the day
   Jerusalem ˹was captured˺.
   They said, "Tear it down! Tear it down
   to its foundation."
⁸ You destructive people of Babylon,
   blessed is the one who pays you back
   with the same treatment you gave us.
⁹ Blessed is the one who grabs your little children
   and smashes them against a rock.

## PSALM 138

By David.

¹ I will give thanks to you with all my heart.
   I will make music to praise you
   in front of the false gods.
² I will bow toward your holy temple.
   I will give thanks to your name
   because of your mercy and truth.
   You have made your name and your promise
   greater than everything.

³ When I called, you answered me.
   You made me bold by strengthening my soul.ᵃ

---

ᵃ 138:3 Hebrew meaning of this line uncertain.

4   All the kings of the earth will give thanks to you,
        O LORD,
      because they have heard the promises you spoke.
5       They will sing this about the ways of the LORD:
          "The LORD's honor is great!"
6   Even though the LORD is high above,
        he sees humble people ⌞close up⌟,
      and he recognizes arrogant people
        from a distance.

7   Even though I walk into the middle of trouble,
        you guard my life against the anger
          of my enemies.
      You stretch out your hand,
        and your right hand saves me.
8   The LORD will do everything for me.
      O LORD, your mercy endures forever.
      Do not let go of what your hands have made.


### PROVERBS 29:18-27

18  Without prophetic vision people run wild,
        but blessed are those who follow
          ⌞God's⌟ teachings.
19  A slave cannot be disciplined with words.
        He will not respond, though he may understand.
20  Have you met a person who is quick to answer?
        There is more hope for a fool than for him.
21  Pamper a slave from childhood,
        and later he will be ungrateful.[a]

22  An angry person stirs up a fight,
        and a hothead does much wrong.

---

[a] 29:21 Hebrew meaning uncertain.

23 A person's pride will humiliate him,
    but a humble spirit gains honor.
24 Whoever is a thief's partner hates his own life.
    He will not testify under oath.
25 A person's fear sets a trap ₍for him₎,
    but one who trusts the LORD is safe.
26 Many seek an audience with a ruler,
    but justice for humanity comes from the LORD.
27 An unjust person is disgusting to righteous people.
    A decent person is disgusting to wicked people.


# *Day 85* ≈

## PSALM 139

For the choir director; a psalm by David.

1 O LORD, you have examined me, and you know me.
2     You alone know when I sit down
            and when I get up.
    You read my thoughts from far away.
3     You watch me when I travel and when I rest.
    You are familiar with all my ways.
4         Even before there is a ₍single₎ word
                on my tongue,
            you know all about it, LORD.
5     You are all around me—in front of me
            and in back of me.
    You lay your hand on me.
6         Such knowledge is beyond my grasp.
            It is so high I cannot reach it.

7   Where can I go ˌto get awayˌ from your Spirit?
    Where can I run ˌto get awayˌ from you?
8      If I go up to heaven, you are there.
       If I make my bed in hell, you are there.
9      If I climb upward on the rays of the morning sun
          ˌorˌ land on the most distant shore of the sea
             where the sun sets,
10            even there your hand would guide me
                 and your right hand would hold on to me.
11     If I say, "Let the darkness hide me
          and let the light around me turn into night,"
12            even the darkness is not too dark for you.
                 Night is as bright as day.
                 Darkness and light are the same ˌto youˌ.


13  You alone created my inner being.
    You knitted me together inside my mother.
14  I will give thanks to you
       because I have been so amazingly
          and miraculously made.
          Your works are miraculous,
             and my soul is fully aware of this.
15  My bones were not hidden from you
       when I was being made in secret,
       when I was being skillfully woven
          in an underground workshop.
16  Your eyes saw me when I was only a fetus.
       Every day ˌof my lifeˌ was recorded in your book
          before one of them had taken place.
17  How precious are your thoughts concerning me,
       O God!
    How vast in number they are!
18     If I try to count them,

there would be more of them
than there are grains of sand.
When I wake up, I am still with you.

19 I wish that you would kill wicked people, O God,
and that bloodthirsty people
would leave me alone.
20 They say wicked things about you.
Your enemies misuse your name.
21 Shouldn't I hate those who hate you, O LORD?
Shouldn't I be disgusted with those who attack you?
22 I hate them with all my heart.
They have become my enemies.

23 Examine me, O God, and know my mind.
Test me, and know my thoughts.
24 See whether I am on an evil path.
Then lead me on the everlasting path.


## PROVERBS 30:1-9

1 The words of Agur, son of Jakeh. Agur's prophetic
revelation.

### Agur Speaks About God

[To God]
This man's declaration:
"I'm weary, O God.
I'm weary and worn out, O God.
2 I'm more ⸤like⸥ a dumb animal
than a human being.
I don't ⸤even⸥ have human understanding.

<sup>3</sup>      I haven't learned wisdom.
I don't have knowledge of the Holy One.[a]

**[To the audience]**

<sup>4</sup>   "Who has gone up to heaven and come down?
Who has gathered the wind in the palm of his hand?
Who has wrapped water in a garment?
Who has set up the earth from one end
     to the other?
What is his name or the name of his son?
     Certainly, you must know!

<sup>5</sup>   "Every word of God has proven to be true.
He is a shield to those who come to him
     for protection.

<sup>6</sup>   Do not add to his words,
or he will reprimand you,
     and you will be found to be a liar.

### A Prayer

**[To God]**

<sup>7</sup>   "I've asked you for two things.
Don't keep them from me before I die:

<sup>8</sup>     Keep vanity and lies far away from me.
Don't give me either poverty or riches.
Feed me ˻only˼ the food I need,

<sup>9</sup>        or I may feel satisfied and deny you
and say, 'Who is the LORD?'
or I may become poor and steal
and give the name of my God
a bad reputation.

---

[a] 30:3 Or "holy ones."

# *Day 86* ≈

## PSALM 140

For the choir leader; a psalm by David.

1   Rescue me from evil people, O LORD.
    Keep me safe from violent people.
2      They plan evil things in their hearts.
      They start fights every day.
3      They make their tongues
         as sharp as a snake's ⌊fang⌋.
     Their lips hide the venom of poisonous snakes.

                                    *Selah*

4   Protect me from the hands of wicked people,
      O LORD.
    Keep me safe from violent people.
     They try to trip me.
5   Arrogant people have laid a trap for me.
     They have spread out a net with ropes.
     They have set traps for me along the road.    *Selah*

6   I said to the LORD, "You are my God."
     O LORD, open your ears to hear my plea for pity.
7      O LORD Almighty, the strong one who saves me,
      you have covered my head in the day of battle.
8      O LORD, do not give wicked people what they want.
      Do not let their evil plans succeed,
        ⌊or⌋ they will become arrogant.      *Selah*

9   Let the heads of those who surround me
     be covered with their own threats.

<sup>10</sup> Let burning coals fall on them.
    Let them be thrown into a pit, never to rise again.
<sup>11</sup> Do not let slanderers prosper on earth.
    Let evil hunt down violent people
        with one blow after another.

<sup>12</sup> I know that the LORD will defend the rights
        of those who are oppressed
    and the cause of those who are needy.
<sup>13</sup>     Indeed, righteous people will give thanks
        to your name.
    Decent people will live in your presence.

## PSALM 141

A psalm by David.

<sup>1</sup> O LORD, I cry out to you, "Come quickly."
    Open your ears to me when I cry out to you.
<sup>2</sup> Let my prayer be accepted
    as sweet-smelling incense in your presence.
    Let the lifting up of my hands in prayer be accepted
        as an evening sacrifice.

<sup>3</sup> O LORD, set a guard at my mouth.
    Keep watch over the door of my lips.
<sup>4</sup> Do not let me be persuaded to do anything evil
        or to become involved with wickedness,
        with people who are troublemakers.
        Do not let me taste their delicacies.

<sup>5</sup> A righteous person may strike me or correct me
        out of kindness.
    It is like lotion for my head.
        My head will not refuse it,

. because my prayer is directed
              against evil deeds.
6   When their judges are thrown off a cliff,
        they will listen to what I have to say.
        It will sound pleasant ˛to them˛.
7   As someone plows and breaks up the ground,
        so our bones will be planted at the mouth
              of the grave.ᵃ

8   My eyes look to you, LORD Almighty.
    I have taken refuge in you.
        Do not leave me defenseless.
9       Keep me away from the trap they set for me
              and from the traps set by troublemakers.
10      Let wicked people fall into their own nets,
              while I escape unharmed.


                        PSALM 142

A *maskil*ᵇ by David when he was in the cave; a prayer.

1   Loudly, I cry to the LORD.
    Loudly, I plead with the LORD for mercy.
2       I pour out my complaints in his presence
              and tell him my troubles.
3           When I begin to lose hope,
                  you ˛already˛ know what I am experiencing.

    ˛My enemies˛ have hidden a trap for me on the path
        where I walk.
4   Look to my right and see that no one notices me.
        Escape is impossible for me.
              No one cares about me.

---

ᵃ 141:7 Hebrew meaning of verses 5–7 uncertain.   ᵇ 142:1 Unknown musical term.

5    I call out to you, O LORD.
     I say, "You are my refuge,
        my own inheritance in this world of the living."
6    Pay attention to my cry for help
       because I am very weak.
     Rescue me from those who pursue me
       because they are too strong for me.
7    Release my soul from prison
       so that I may give thanks to your name.
       Righteous people will surround me
         because you are good to me.

## PROVERBS 30:10-20

### Against Slander

**[To the audience]**
10    "Do not slander a slave to his master.
       The slave will curse you,
        and you will be found guilty."

### Four Kinds of People

11    A certain kind of person curses his father
       and does not bless his mother.
12    A certain kind of person thinks he is pure
       but is not washed from his own feces.[a]
13    A certain kind of person looks around arrogantly
       and is conceited.
14    A certain kind of person,
       whose teeth are like swords
        and whose jaws are ˻like˼ knives,
         devours oppressed people from the earth
         and people from among humanity.

---

[a] 30:12 Blunt Hebrew term but not considered vulgar.

### Human Bloodsuckers

<sup></sup>**15**  The bloodsucking leech has two daughters—
   "Give!" and "Give!"

### Four Things That Are Never Satisfied

Three things are never satisfied.
Four never say, "Enough!":
**16**  the grave,
   a barren womb,
   a land that never gets enough water,
   a fire that does not say, "Enough!"

### Disrespectful Children—Their Punishment

**17**  The eye that makes fun of a father
   and hates to obey a mother
will be plucked out by ravens in the valley
   and eaten by young vultures.

### Four Things of Intrigue

**18**  Three things are too amazing to me,
even four that I cannot understand:
**19**  an eagle making its way through the sky,
   a snake making its way over a rock,
   a ship making its way through high seas,
   a man making his way with a virgin.

### About the Woman Who Commits Adultery

**20**  This is the way of a woman who commits adultery:
   She eats, wipes her mouth,
      and says, "I haven't done anything wrong!"

# *Day 87* ≈

## PSALM 143

A psalm by David.

1   O LORD, listen to my prayer.
     Open your ears to hear my urgent requests.
     Answer me because you are faithful and righteous.

2   Do not take me to court for judgment,
     because there is no one alive
       who is righteous in your presence.

3   The enemy has pursued me.
     He has ground my life into the dirt.
     He has made me live in dark places
       like those who have died long ago.

4   That is why I begin to lose hope
     and my heart is in a state of shock.

5   I remember the days long ago.
     I reflect on all that you have done.
     I carefully consider what your hands have made.

6   I stretch out my hands to you in prayer.
     Like parched land, my soul thirsts for you.    *Selah*

7   Answer me quickly, O LORD.
     My spirit is worn out.
  Do not hide your face from me,
     or I will be like those who go into the pit.

8   Let me hear about your mercy in the morning,
     because I trust you.
  Let me know the way that I should go,

because I long for you.
9 Rescue me from my enemies, O LORD.
I come to you for protection.

10 Teach me to do your will, because you are my God.
May your good Spirit lead me on level ground.
11 O LORD, keep me alive for the sake of your name.
Because you are righteous, lead me out of trouble.
12 In keeping with your mercy, wipe out my enemies
and destroy all who torment me,
because I am your servant.

## PSALM 144

By David.

1 Thank the LORD, my rock,
who trained my hands to fight
and my fingers to do battle,
2 my merciful one, my fortress,
my stronghold, and my savior,
my shield, the one in whom I take refuge,
and the one who brings people
under my authority.

3 O LORD, what are humans
that you should care about them?
What are mere mortals
that you should think about them?
4 Humans are like a breath of air.
Their life span is like a fleeting shadow.

5 O LORD, bend your heaven low, and come down.
Touch the mountains, and they will smoke.
6 Hurl bolts of lightning, and scatter them.

Shoot your arrows, and throw them
    into confusion.

7 Stretch out your hands from above.
Snatch me, and rescue me from raging waters
    and from foreigners' hands.

8     Their mouths speak lies.
    Their right hands take false pledges.

9 O God, I will sing a new song to you.
    I will sing a psalm to you on a ten-stringed harp.

10 You are the one who gives victory to kings.
You are the one who snatches your servant David
    away from a deadly sword.

11     Snatch me, and rescue me
        from foreigners' hands.
    Their mouths speak lies.
    Their right hands take false pledges.

12 May our sons be like full-grown, young plants.
May our daughters be like stately columns
    that adorn the corners of a palace.

13 May our barns be filled with all kinds of crops.
May our sheep give birth to thousands of lambs,
    tens of thousands in our fields.

14 May our cattle have many calves.[a]

May no one break in,
    and may no one be dragged out.
May there be no cries of distress in our streets.

15     Blessed are the people who have these blessings!
    Blessed are the people whose God is the LORD!

---

[a] 144:14 Hebrew meaning of this verse uncertain.

## PROVERBS 30:21-33

### Four Things That Are Intolerable

21 Three things cause the earth to tremble,
even four it cannot bear up under:
22 a slave when he becomes king,
a godless fool when he is filled with food,
23 a woman who is unloved when she gets married,
a maid when she replaces her mistress.

### Four Things That Are Small—Yet Smart and Strong

24 Four things on earth are small,
yet they are very wise:
25 Ants are not a strong species,
yet they store their food in summer.
26 Rock badgers are not a mighty species,
yet they make their home in the rocks.
27 Locusts have no king,
yet all of them divide into swarms by instinct.
28 A lizard you can hold in your hands,
yet it can even be found in royal palaces.

### Four Things That Move With Dignity

29 There are three things that walk with dignity,
even four that march with dignity:
30 a lion, mightiest among animals,
which turns away from nothing,
31 a strutting rooster,*a*
a male goat,
a king at the head of his army.*b*

---

*a* 30:31 Hebrew meaning of this line uncertain.   *b* 30:31 Hebrew meaning of "at the head of his army" uncertain.

**Keep Calm and Quiet**

<sup>32</sup> If you are such a godless fool as to honor yourself,
or if you scheme,
you had better put your hand over your mouth.
<sup>33</sup> As churning milk produces butter
and punching a nose produces blood,
so stirring up anger[a] produces a fight.

### PSALM 145[b]

A song of praise by David.

<sup>1</sup> I will highly praise you, my God, the king.
I will bless your name forever and ever.
<sup>2</sup> I will bless you every day.
I will praise your name forever and ever.

<sup>3</sup> The LORD is great, and he should be highly praised.
His greatness is unsearchable.
<sup>4</sup> One generation will praise your deeds to the next.
Each generation will talk about your mighty acts.
<sup>5</sup> I will think about the glorious honor of your majesty
and the miraculous things you have done.
<sup>6</sup> People will talk about the power
of your terrifying deeds,
and I will tell about your greatness.

---

[a] 30:33 In Hebrew there is a play on words in verse 33 where the same verb is used to express all three actions. [b] 145:1 Psalm 145 is a poem in Hebrew alphabetical order.

7   They will announce what they remember
        of your great goodness,
      and they will joyfully sing
        about your righteousness.
8   The LORD is merciful, compassionate, patient,
      and always ready to forgive.
9   The LORD is good to everyone
      and has compassion for everything
        that he has made.
10  Everything that you have made
      will give thanks to you, O LORD,
      and your faithful ones will praise you.
11  Everyone will talk about the glory of your kingdom
      and will tell the descendants of Adam
        about your might
12        in order to make known your mighty deeds
        and the glorious honor of your kingdom.
13  Your kingdom is an everlasting kingdom.
    Your empire endures throughout every generation.

14  The LORD supports everyone who falls.
    He straightens ˌthe backsˏ of those
        who are bent over.
15      The eyes of all creatures look to you,
        and you give them their food
            at the proper time.
16      You open your hand,
        and you satisfy the desire of every living thing.
17  The LORD is fair in all his ways
      and faithful in everything he does.
18  The LORD is near to everyone who prays to him,
      to every faithful person who prays to him.
19  He fills the needs of those who fear him.

He hears their cries for help and saves them.
20 The LORD protects everyone who loves him,
  but he will destroy all wicked people.

21 My mouth will speak the praise of the LORD,
  and all living creatures will praise his holy name
    forever and ever.

## PROVERBS 31:1-9

1 The sayings of King Lemuel, a prophetic revelation,
  used by his mother to discipline him.

### Advice to a Prince

2 "What, my son?
  What, son to whom I gave birth?
  What, son of my prayers?
3   Don't give your strength to women
    or your power to those who ruin kings.

4 "It is not for kings, Lemuel.
  It is not for kings to drink wine
    or for rulers to crave liquor.
5   Otherwise, they drink
      and forget what they have decreed
    and change the standard of justice
      for all oppressed people.
6 Give liquor to a person who is dying
  and wine to one who feels resentful.
7   Such a person drinks
    and forgets his poverty
    and does not remember
      his trouble anymore.

8 "Speak out for the one who cannot speak,
   for the rights of those who are doomed.
9 Speak out,
      judge fairly,
         and defend the rights of oppressed
            and needy people."

# Day 89 ❧

## PSALM 146

1 Hallelujah!

Praise the LORD, my soul!
2 I want to praise the LORD throughout my life.
   I want to make music to praise my God
      as long as I live.

3 Do not trust influential people,
      mortals who cannot help you.
4       When they breathe their last breath,
            they return to the ground.
               On that day their plans come to an end.
5 Blessed are those who receive help
      from the God of Jacob.
   Their hope rests on the LORD their God,
6       who made heaven, earth,
            the sea, and everything in them.
   The LORD remains faithful forever.
7 He brings about justice for those
      who are oppressed.
   He gives food to those who are hungry.

The L ORD sets prisoners free.
8    The L ORD gives sight to blind people.
The L ORD straightens ˌthe backsˌ of those
who are bent over.
The L ORD loves righteous people.
9    The L ORD protects foreigners.
The L ORD gives relief to orphans and widows.
But he keeps wicked people
from reaching their goal.
10   The L ORD rules as king forever.
Zion, your God rules throughout every generation.

Hallelujah!


## PSALM 147

1    Hallelujah!

It is good to sing psalms to our God.
It is pleasant to sing ˌhisˌ praise beautifully.

2    The L ORD is the builder of Jerusalem.
He is the one who gathers the outcasts
of Israel together.
3        He is the healer of the brokenhearted.
He is the one who bandages their wounds.
4        He determines the number of stars.
He gives each one a name.
5    Our Lord is great, and his power is great.
There is no limit to his understanding.
6    The L ORD gives relief to those who are oppressed.
He brings wicked people down to the ground.

7    Sing to the L ORD a song of thanksgiving.
Make music to our God with a lyre.

8    He covers the sky with clouds.
     He provides rain for the ground.
     He makes grass grow on the mountains.
9    He is the one who gives food to animals
          and to young ravens when they call out.
10   He finds no joy in strong horses,
          nor is he pleased by brave soldiers.
11   The LORD is pleased with those who fear him,
          with those who wait with hope for his mercy.

12   Praise the LORD, Jerusalem!
     Praise your God, Zion!
13   He makes the bars across your gates strong.
     He blesses the children within you.
14   He is the one who brings peace to your borders
          and satisfies your ⸢hunger⸣ with the finest wheat.
15   He is the one who sends his promise
               throughout the earth.
     His word travels with great speed.
16   He is the one who sends snow like wool
          and scatters frost like ashes.
17   He is the one who throws his hailstones
               like breadcrumbs.
     Who can withstand his chilling blast?
18   He sends out his word and melts his hailstones.
     He makes wind blow ⸢and⸣ water flow.
19   He speaks his word to Jacob,
          his laws and judicial decisions to Israel.
20   He has done nothing like this for any other nation.
          The other nations do not know the decisions
               he has handed down.

     Hallelujah!

### PROVERBS 31:10-22

#### A *Poem in Hebrew Alphabetical Order*

10  "Who can find a wife with a strong character?
    She is worth far more than jewels.
11  Her husband trusts her with ˻all˼ his heart,
    and he does not lack anything good.
12  She helps him and never harms him all the days
        of her life.

13  "She seeks out wool and linen ˻with care˼
    and works with willing hands.
14  She is like merchant ships.
    She brings her food from far away.
15  She wakes up while it is still dark
        and gives food to her family
            and portions of food to her female slaves.

16  "She picks out a field and buys it.
    She plants a vineyard
        from the profits she has earned.
17  She puts on strength like a belt
    and goes to work with energy.
18  She sees that she is making a good profit.
    Her lamp burns late at night.

19  "She puts her hands on the distaff,
    and her fingers hold a spindle.
20  She opens her hands to oppressed people
    and stretches them out to needy people.
21  She does not fear for her family when it snows
        because her whole family
            has a double layer of clothing.
22  She makes quilts for herself.
    Her clothes are ˻made of˼ linen and purple cloth.

# *Day 90* ≈

## PSALM 148

¹ Hallelujah!

Praise the LORD from the heavens.
Praise him in the heights above.
² Praise him, all his angels.
Praise him, his entire heavenly army.
³ Praise him, sun and moon.
Praise him, all shining stars.
⁴ Praise him, you highest heaven
and the water above the sky.
⁵ Let them praise the name of the LORD
because they were created by his command.
⁶ He set them in their places forever and ever.
He made it a law that no one can break.

⁷ Praise the LORD from the earth.
Praise him, large sea creatures
and all the ocean depths,
⁸ lightning and hail,
snow and fog,
strong winds that obey his commands,
⁹ mountains and all hills,
fruit trees and all cedar trees,
¹⁰ wild animals and all domestic animals,
crawling animals and birds,
¹¹ kings of the earth and all its people,
officials and all judges on the earth,
¹² young men and women,

old and young together.

¹³ Let them praise the name of the LORD
because his name is high above all others.
His glory is above heaven and earth.

¹⁴ He has given his people a strong leader,[a]
someone praiseworthy for his faithful ones,
for the people of Israel,
the people who are close to him.

Hallelujah!

## PSALM 149

¹ Hallelujah!

Sing a new song to the LORD.
Sing his praise in the assembly of godly people.

² Let Israel find joy in their creator.
Let the people of Zion rejoice over their king.

³ Let them praise his name with dancing.
Let them make music to him
with tambourines and lyres,

⁴ because the LORD takes pleasure in his people.
He crowns those who are oppressed
with victory.

⁵ Let godly people triumph in glory.
Let them sing for joy on their beds.

⁶ Let the high praises of God be in their throats
and two-edged swords in their hands

⁷ to take vengeance on the nations,
to punish the people of the world,

⁸ to put their kings in chains
and their leaders in iron shackles,

---

[a] 148:14 Or "given his people strength."

9         to carry out the judgment
            that is written against them.
        This is an honor that belongs
            to all his godly ones.

Hallelujah!

## PSALM 150

1  Hallelujah!

Praise God in his holy place.
Praise him in his mighty heavens.
2  Praise him for his mighty acts.
Praise him for his immense greatness.
3  Praise him with sounds from horns.
Praise him with harps and lyres.
4  Praise him with tambourines and dancing.
Praise him with stringed instruments and flutes.
5  Praise him with loud cymbals.
Praise him with crashing cymbals.

6  Let everything that breathes praise the Lord!

Hallelujah!

## PROVERBS 31:23-31

23  "Her husband is known at the city gates
    when he sits with the leaders of the land.

24  "She makes linen garments and sells them
    and delivers belts to the merchants.
25  She dresses with strength and nobility,
    and she smiles at the future.

26    "She speaks with wisdom,
          and on her tongue there is tender instruction.
27    She keeps a close eye on the conduct of her family,
          and she does not eat the bread of idleness.
28    Her children and her husband
          stand up and bless her.
      In addition, he sings her praises, by saying,
29        'Many women have done noble work,
              but you have surpassed them all!'

30    "Charm is deceptive, and beauty evaporates,
          ⌊but⌋ a woman who has the fear of the LORD
              should be praised.
31    Reward her for what she has done,
          and let her achievements praise her
              at the city gates."